Department of the Environment, Transport and the Regions

The Channel Tunnel Rail Link

REPORT BY THE COMPTROLLER AND AUDITOR GENERAL
HC 302 Session 2000-2001: 28 March 2001

LONDON: The Stationery Office
£11.50

10 305 8531

Ordered by the
House of Commons
to be printed on 26 March 2001

This report has been prepared under Section 6 of the National Audit Act 1983 for presentation to the House of Commons in accordance with Section 9 of the Act.

John Bourn   **National Audit Office**
Comptroller and Auditor General   **22 March 2001**

The Comptroller and Auditor General is the head of the National Audit Office employing some 750 staff. He, and the National Audit Office, are totally independent of Government. He certifies the accounts of all Government departments and a wide range of other public sector bodies; and he has statutory authority to report to Parliament on the economy, efficiency and effectiveness with which departments and other bodies have used their resources.

For further information about the National Audit Office please contact:

National Audit Office
Press Office
157-197 Buckingham Palace Road
Victoria
London
SW1W 9SP

Tel: 020 7798 7400

Email: enquiries@nao.gsi.gov.uk
Website address: www.nao.gov.uk

Contents

Executive summary   1

Part 1

To ensure completion of the Link, the   11
Department allowed the original deal to evolve

Poorer than expected performance of Eurostar UK   11
put the original deal at risk

The original deal came close to collapsing   14

The Department wanted the Link completed without   16
a material increase in the direct grants

The restructured deal is in many respects more   17
robust than the original

Part 2

The complex financing of the Link requires   21
long-term Government support

The Link will be financed from a complex mixture   21
of public and private finance and guarantees

The decision to use Government-guaranteed bonds   24
was finely balanced

The taxpayer faces both open-ended financial risks   26
and the possibility of returns

Part 3

The case for public sector support is heavily   29
dependent on wider benefits

Public sector support for the Link was inevitable   29

The Department estimated that the economic and   31
wider benefits would outweigh the subsidy, so support
for the Link was economically justified

The Department's economic assessment of the project   33
is debatable

Appendices

1. Chronology of key events   38

2. Scope and methodology of the National Audit   39
   Office's examination

3. Additional information on the Link   40

4. Advisers for the restructuring of the project   45

5. Evaluation of funding of LCR   46

6. Pricing of public transport services with   76
   high capital costs

7. Financial and cost-benefit analysis framework   77

8. The key benefits and costs included in the value   81
   for money assessment of the link

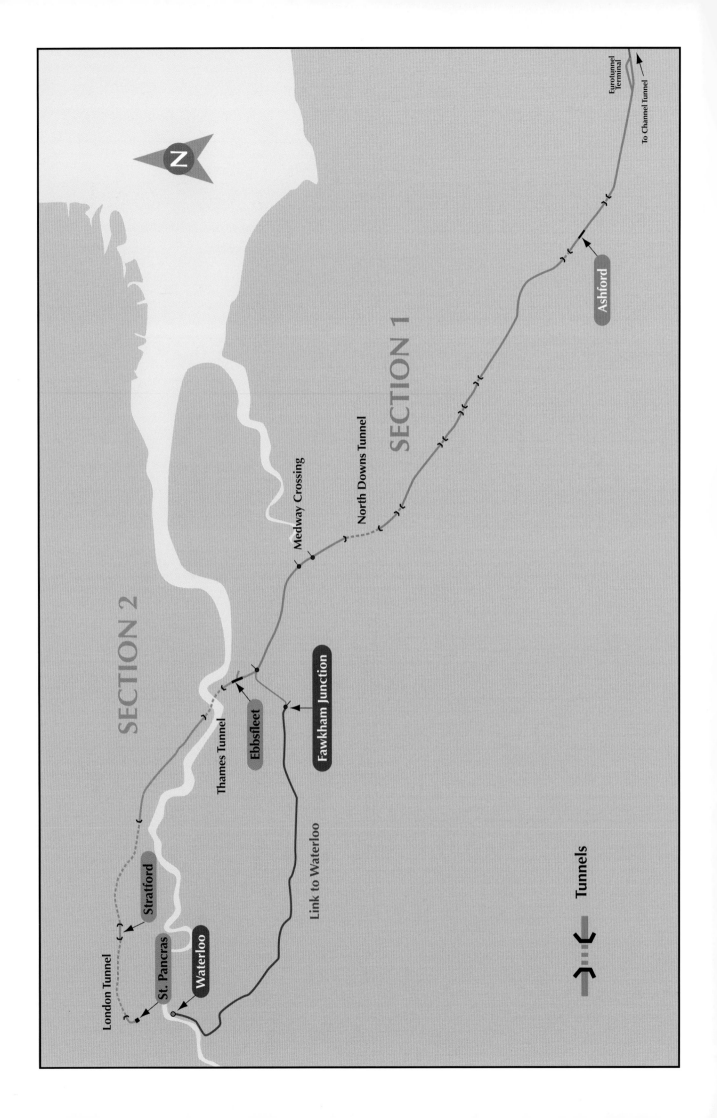

executive summary

In this section

Why the Department   2
restructured the deal

Public expenditure impacts 3

The economic justification 6
for public sector support

Lessons learned   8

1   The contract under the Private Finance Initiative to build the Channel Tunnel Rail Link (the Link) and run the UK arm of the Eurostar international train service (Eurostar UK) was awarded to London & Continental Railways Limited (LCR) in February 1996. The contract was in line with the principles of the Private Finance Initiative: it envisaged that LCR would finance, build and operate the Link drawing revenue primarily from Eurostar UK and from use of the Link by domestic train services. The Department of the Environment, Transport and the Regions (the Department) agreed to provide LCR with direct grants totalling £1,730[1] million for the construction of the Link and its use by domestic train services. It was expected that construction would start in 1998 and that the Link would open in 2003.

2   At the end of 1997 it had become clear that overly optimistic forecasts for the operating performance of Eurostar UK had scuppered LCR's efforts to raise all the money it needed from private investors to build the Link. In January 1998, the company therefore asked for an additional £1,200 million[2] in direct grants from the Department. Following negotiations, the Deputy Prime Minister announced in June 1998 that the Department had agreed with LCR on a way forward which would not involve a material increase in the direct grants to be paid to LCR. However, it did involve a radical restructuring of the project and the role of LCR. A chronology of key events is at Appendix 1.

3   The restructured deal retains the same route for the Link but splits construction into two sections: Section 1, from the Channel Tunnel to near Ebbsfleet on the outskirts of London and Section 2, from near Ebbsfleet to St. Pancras. Railtrack has been brought in both to manage construction and, when it is completed, to purchase Section 1. Railtrack also has an option to purchase Section 2 on the same basis. Construction of Section 1 began in October 1998 and is on target for completion by 30 September 2003. Completion of the entire Link is now scheduled for late 2006. The financing of the restructured project is fundamentally different to that envisaged in 1996, and so is the distribution of risks among the various parties now involved with the deal.

---

1   Future cashflows in the original deal were evaluated at 1995 prices, discounted at 6 per cent real to 1995.

2   To allow comparison with the original deal, LCR's request for additional direct grants of £1,200 million was expressed in 1995 prices, discounted at 6 per cent real to 1995. When expressed in 1997 prices, discounted at 6 per cent real to 1997, the figure increases to £1,294 million.

4 This report examines:

a) the Department's reasons for restructuring the deal rather than choosing other options;

b) the likely implications of the restructured deal for public expenditure; and

c) the justification for the direct grants which the Link will require.

Our methodology is summarised at Appendix 2.

Why the Department restructured the deal

5 The original deal combined construction of the Link with the privatisation of what was at the time a relatively new Eurostar UK train service to Paris and Brussels. It rested on LCR's forecasts that Eurostar UK would grow quickly enough for the revenues generated to support the raising of private finance to cover the heavy costs of constructing the Link. Ahead of a main finance raising exercise, the Department agreed to support initial borrowing by LCR of over £400 million from a syndicate of banks. LCR's original shareholders put up £60 million of equity finance (*paragraphs 1.1 to 1.10*).

6 In the event, Eurostar UK performed much less well than expected and LCR was unable to continue on the original plan. The Department encouraged LCR to seek other ways of carrying on with the project, and LCR held initial discussions with Railtrack in 1997. Finding that it was not possible to reach agreement with Railtrack LCR approached the Government seeking additional direct grants, before its finances were exhausted (*paragraphs 1.11 to 1.26*).

7 The Department rejected the option of simply agreeing to pay additional grants and made it clear to LCR that it wanted the Link completed without a material increase in the size of the direct grants. The Department was also unwilling to dispense with LCR and begin the process of selecting a private sector partner all over again. Such a move would have involved a further delay of at least two years and prolonged the planning blight, which had affected properties near the route of the Link (*paragraphs 1.27 to 1.32*).

8 The Department therefore decided to restructure the deal with LCR. The Department's key objectives for the restructuring were:

a) to ensure that the Link would be built without a material increase in the level of direct grants agreed in the original deal;

b) to inject new private sector management into Eurostar UK;

c) to ensure that the parties to a restructured deal would be financially committed to it and financially strong enough to meet their obligations; and

d) to achieve a true Public Private Partnership with each risk allocated to the party best able to manage it and with rewards commensurate with the risks.

9 The Department achieved its key objectives during the restructuring and the restructured deal is in many respects more robust than the original:

financing the construction of the first Section of the Link is no longer dependent on the performance of Eurostar UK

a) Apart from payments of direct grants, the finance for Section 1 now comes from two sources: commercial bank borrowing by LCR which has been guaranteed by Railtrack, and an issue of bonds by LCR which carry a Government guarantee (*paragraph 1.34*).

construction risk remains with the private sector

b) Because Railtrack will manage the construction of Section 1 and purchase it at a price linked to the actual cost of construction, the construction risk was allocated to a party that was considered capable of managing it and was strong enough to meet the financial obligations involved (*paragraphs 1.35 to 1.37*).

there are improved arrangements for sharing Eurostar UK revenue risk

c) Eurostar UK is now being managed by a private sector company appointed by LCR, Inter Capital and Regional Railways Limited (ICRR). The management fee paid to ICRR is a percentage of Eurostar UK turnover, adjusted by a sharing of operating cashflow risk with LCR (*paragraphs 1.38 to 1.40*).

the Department has improved its monitoring of the project

d) Under the original deal, the Department decided not to demand all the information it was entitled to under the contract with LCR. This decision hampered the Department's ability to monitor progress and at the same time denied the external financiers at the early stages of the project the opportunity to bring private sector financial disciplines to the deal. In the restructured deal, the Department now has considerable influence on the way the whole project is being managed. It has a special share in ICRR; it is a co-signatory to the contract between Railtrack and LCR and the Department has appointed a director to the board of LCR. In addition, the Department is actively monitoring the performance of LCR and the other parties to the project (*paragraphs 1.41 and 1.42*).

financing for Section 2 of the Link is yet to be secured

e) Railtrack has an option to purchase Section 2, but no obligation to construct it. LCR is contractually committed to construct Section 2, but may not offer the right to acquire Section 2 to anyone other than Railtrack prior to the expiry of the option in 2003 or Railtrack's agreement to surrender it earlier. As a private sector company reliant on its trading income from the Link, LCR cannot guarantee to be able to raise the necessary finance for Section 2 when it is required (*paragraphs 1.43 to 1.45*).

f) The Department is discussing the arrangements for Section 2 of the Link with LCR, Railtrack and other parties with the intention of concluding a deal very soon. The National Audit Office is monitoring developments and may report further if necessary (*paragraph 1.46*).

Public expenditure impacts

10 In restructuring the deal, the Department avoided any material increase in the net amount of direct grant payable to the project. Nevertheless, the restructured deal now depends on the Government having issued various guarantees and undertakings to lend money directly to LCR. This means that the taxpayer is exposed to considerable financial risk if Eurostar UK does not perform as well as expected against revised forecasts. Set against that risk, the Department will share in any long-term profits if the business is successful.

11 The Link will be financed from a complex mixture of public and private finance and guarantees:

a) In the short term, and beginning during the re-negotiations, LCR conducted a sale-and-leaseback of eleven of its Eurostar train sets, with the Government guaranteeing LCR's obligations amounting to £230 million, pending the arrangement of long-term finance (*paragraph 2.2*);

b) LCR has raised long-term finance of £2,650 million and expects to raise a further £1,100 million through the issue of Government-guaranteed bonds. LCR took the view that an issue of equity would not succeed, and that it would not be practicable to borrow such a large sum from banks. Our advisers, RBC Dominion Securities agree that the bonds represented good value in terms of the rates of interest payable, compared with what was available in the loan markets at the time (*paragraphs 2.4 to 2.6*).

c) Railtrack is obliged to buy Section 1 from LCR, and has guaranteed part of LCR's borrowing. Railtrack will pay the actual cost of construction, including an allowance for the interest costs incurred by LCR, less the direct grants to be paid by the Department to LCR. Railtrack has also guaranteed up to £700 million of commercial bank borrowing by LCR for the specific purpose of financing the construction of Section 1 (*paragraphs 2.7 and 2.8*).

d) In addition to direct grants, the Department has guaranteed payments from Eurostar UK to Railtrack and has provided a capped loan facility for LCR to draw on, depending on how Eurostar UK performs in the future. Direct grants under the restructured deal of £2,010 million[3] will be paid towards the construction and operating costs of the Link. In addition, the Department has guaranteed the payments Eurostar UK will be due to pay Railtrack as owner of Section 1. These "track access charges" are based on the same principles as those applying to the payments by other train operating companies for the use of Railtrack's infrastructure elsewhere on the railway system. In this deal, however, they are also the mechanism by which Railtrack will make a commercial return on its investment in Section 1 (*paragraphs 2.9 to 2.12*).

e) The original shareholders with a continued interest in LCR have converted most of their equity stake into preference shares carrying a fixed rate of interest. One half of these preference shares will be repaid with accrued interest on completion of Section 1 and the other half on completion of the entire Link. LCR's original shareholders did not therefore lose their original investment and did not contribute any further equity to the project (*paragraphs 2.13 to 2.15*).

12 The decision to use Government-guaranteed bonds was finely balanced. The Department considered that their use had advantages over the alternative of making voted loans to LCR, financed through the issue of conventional Government bonds (Gilts):

a) the concept of the Link as a flagship Public Private Partnership would be maintained;

b) it would avoid signalling to other potential PPP developers that the Government would be willing to take on financing risk; and

c) it would keep the project off the public sector balance sheet. This last point depended on the guaranteed bonds not being classified as public sector borrowing, which followed from the Office for National Statistics being satisfied that there was a very low likelihood of the guarantee ever being called (*paragraphs 2.16 to 2.18*).

13 The use of Government-guaranteed bonds will, however, lead to extra funding costs by comparison with Gilts because the interest rates at which they were issued were higher than those of directly comparable Gilts. Our advisers consider that the marketing of the bonds appears to have been handled most carefully and attribute this extra cost to technical factors affecting demand from investors for the bonds. Nevertheless, the advantages over Gilts that the Department saw in using Government-guaranteed bonds were secured at a cost of some £80 million[4] (*paragraphs 2.19 to 2.24*).

14 As a result of the financing structure now put in place for the Link, the taxpayer remains exposed to the financial risks of LCR's business. If Eurostar UK continues to under-perform, the arrangements made for the Government to lend LCR the money to pay Railtrack's access charges would be triggered when LCR's other cash resources, including the money raised from the Government - guaranteed bonds, are exhausted. Scenarios considered by the Department at the time of the restructuring show that between 2010 and 2021 a shortfall ranging from nil to £360 million might arise. A more recent forecast of Eurostar UK performance suggested a range of £360 million to as much as £1,200 million under extreme circumstances. Further, but much smaller, financial exposure will arise from any future Government guarantees of LCR's potential liabilities through a highly complex series of swap transactions, which were used to hedge LCR's risks from changes in interest rates (*paragraphs 2.25 to 2.32*).

15 In restructuring the deal, however, the Department ensured that the taxpayer stood to benefit in the event of Eurostar UK being successful in attracting increased patronage. LCR is not permitted to pay dividends to its shareholders until 2021, but if Eurostar UK does well that restriction could be relaxed before then, provided all accumulated borrowing has been repaid. After 2021, the Government will be entitled to 35 per cent of LCR's pre-tax cashflow and, if LCR is sold or floated, the Government would receive 90 per cent of the proceeds (*paragraphs 2.33 and 2.34*).

---

3   *Future cashflows in the restructured deal were evaluated at 1997 prices, discounted at 6 per cent real to 1997. Direct grants (£1,730 million) agreed under the original deal increase to £2,014 million when expressed in 1997 prices, discounted at 6 per cent real to 1997. In the rest of this report, future cashflows are quoted at 1997 prices, discounted at 6 per cent real to 1997, unless indicated otherwise.*

4   *As at February 1999, the date the Government-guaranteed bonds were issued.*

The economic justification for public sector support

16 The Link could not be developed without very active support from the Government at all stages. The Government is necessarily involved through rail regulation, and through the UK's international obligations, notably those relating to the Channel Tunnel. The Government is thereby obliged to provide sufficient infrastructure to allow for forecast demand for the Tunnel to be met, but there is no obligation to provide a high-speed rail link between London and the Tunnel, which is what the Link will be (*paragraphs 3.2 to 3.6*).

17 It was always envisaged that the Link would not be commercially viable without a substantial Government financial contribution. Not only is the Link one of the largest infrastructure projects in Europe, rendering it unlikely that passenger revenues could cover the enormous investment within a commercially acceptable time, but the Link competes directly with other modes of transport, such as airlines, limiting the fares which can be charged. From the start, the Department was clear that it could back the Link, provided that the estimated benefits could be expected to outweigh the financial contribution made to the project by the Government (*paragraphs 3.7 to 3.12*).

18 Throughout the negotiation of the original deal and the restructuring, the Department analysed the economic justification for making the financial contribution needed if the Link was to be built. The Department's calculations confirmed that the estimated economic benefits of the Link outweigh the required subsidy. The main economic benefits comprise reduced journey times for passengers and increased rail capacity, along with expected regeneration benefits arising from the Link attracting jobs to the areas through which it will run (*paragraphs 3.13 to 3.22*).

19 In renegotiating the original deal, the Department made several changes in its methodology for estimating the benefits the Link would generate. In the final assessment the Department excluded benefits to non-UK resident passengers but included an estimate of regeneration benefits amounting to £500 million. The result, in the Department's most likely estimate of future Eurostar UK patronage, showed total benefits of around £3,000 million for a total public sector contribution of some £2,000 million (*paragraphs 3.24 to 3.26 and Figure 19*).

20 It was a new step to include quantified regeneration benefits. Previously in cost-benefit analysis of transport projects, the Department considered that regeneration benefits would be too uncertain to be quantified in money terms, and to the extent that they could be quantified some of this would represent double counting of passenger benefits already included in the assessment. In this case, however, the Department decided that the methodology for calculating regeneration benefits was sufficiently robust to allow their inclusion in the analysis. The estimate was that the Government would be willing to pay £1,000 million through conventional regeneration funding to secure benefits equivalent to those likely to arise from the Link. This figure was then halved to take account of the double counting (*paragraphs 3.27 to 3.29*).

21   In the Department's view, the innovation of quantifying regeneration benefits in money terms as part of this type of analysis was successful. The Department intends to place more emphasis on quantified regeneration benefits in future projects and is undertaking research on guidance as to what form this quantification might take (*paragraph 3.30*).

22 There is room for debate too about the way passenger benefits were taken into account. At the time, the Department did not have explicit guidance for the appraisal of new heavy rail schemes to complement the guidance it had issued for light rail schemes (such as trams). The Department's figures were based on a calculation that the value of time savings to passengers would, on average, be higher than the fares being paid. This would imply that passengers would not be prepared to pay for the full benefits they would get from using the Link (*paragraphs 3.31 to 3.34*).

23   We examined the other key assumptions made in the Department's calculations. In our view, some of them are questionable. Substituting more reasonable assumptions, we have estimated that there would be a net benefit from the Link of under £500 million, and that if money estimates of regeneration benefits are excluded, in line with Departmental guidance, then the net benefits of the project would only be marginal. To the extent that Eurostar UK does not achieve the levels of usage assumed in the Department's most likely estimate of future Eurostar UK patronage, then the costs of on-going public subsidy for the project are likely to be increased and the quantified net benefits of the project are likely to be reduced still further. On the basis of recent Eurostar UK performance, which has been below this level, the Link represents poor value for money in terms of estimated economic benefits (*paragraphs 3.35 to 3.40*).

24 What this means is that the economic justification for Government support for the project rests heavily on wider policy benefits associated with the Link. The Government saw the project as one of national prestige. It will provide a high speed rail service to Europe. France and Belgium already have such high speed connections to the Channel Tunnel, and the Link is one of a number of high priority projects for the development of high speed rail routes across Europe. This has given the Link priority status in the Government's overall transport policy. Although such a consideration was not formally included in the Department's stated objectives, it was an important consideration in Ministerial announcements on the project (*paragraph 3.23*).

executive summary

Lessons learned

25 We cannot comment at this stage on whether the Department's objective to ensure the construction of the entire Link will be achieved. Nevertheless, it is apparent from our examination that, in difficult circumstances, a range of complex issues had to be addressed and that the Department handled the negotiations with LCR in a competent manner. Although the project to build the Link and privatise Eurostar UK is unique in many respects, the conclusions that can be drawn from it are not. There are, therefore, a number of important lessons to be borne in mind for future Public Private Partnerships, along with some specific points for the Department.

Lessons for departments from the structure of the original deal:

Revenue forecasts for start up businesses are subject to great uncertainty

1 There have been several recent examples of high profile start up projects whose business plans have depended on forecasts of usage by members of the public, and these forecasts have turned out to be highly optimistic.[5] As bidders' forecasts of revenues from the fledgling Eurostar UK business were in line with previous estimates made by the Department and British Rail, the Department did not seek to have them independently validated. Moreover, in the absence of proven demand, it was not possible for either party to this deal to be sure that forecast revenues would be sufficient to support LCR's planned stock market flotation. Eurostar UK's poor performance weakened LCR's financial strength to such an extent that its ability to fund the Link was destroyed. As a result the entire project came close to collapse.

Make sure that bidders for a deal are not encouraged to be over-optimistic

2 A key element of the initial competition in 1994-95 to find a promoter for the Link was the level of direct grants required by each bidder. As the level of direct grants would depend on the amount of revenue each bidder thought it could secure from operating Eurostar UK, there was an in-built incentive for bidders to be over-optimistic about the prospects for the business.

The equity capital to be invested in a project should reflect the risks of that project

3 Departments should ensure that the capital structure of a proposed deal is consistent with the risks involved in the project. If the proportion of risk or equity capital is too low, the project will not be financially robust in the face of lower than expected revenues. Moreover, having a relatively low investment at risk may provide insufficient incentive for the private sector shareholders to tackle business problems with determination. Either way, the impact of proceeding with too little risk capital is likely to be a call on the public sector for increased financial support, as happened in this case. It follows that a department should take a close interest in the private sector's proposals as regards the capital structure of Public Private Partnerships. If the market is unwilling to subscribe sufficient equity capital it is a clear signal regarding the riskiness of the project, the implications of which need to be thought through by the department concerned.

---

5   *The Millennium Dome (HC 936/1999-00) and The Re-negotiation of the PFI-type Deal for the Royal Armouries Museum in Leeds (HC 103/2000-01)*

Government guarantees of project debts are unlikely to be costless

4 In signing a direct agreement with LCR's bankers, the Department agreed to support the servicing of all of the £430 million borrowed during the early stages of the project. The effect of this was that, if the agreement with LCR was terminated, the Department agreed to take back not just the assets of the Eurostar UK business but also its outstanding liabilities. The Department therefore retained the risk that future Eurostar UK revenues would be insufficient to service this debt and attract further investment in the project. If the market is unwilling to provide sufficient debt capital secured on the project, that is a clear signal that the project risks go beyond normal commercial risks. A Government guarantee of debt capital transfers project risks to the department, which needs therefore to consider thoroughly how to manage those risks.

Substantial risks arise if public sector assets are transferred in advance of external finance raising

5 In the original deal, significant public sector assets were transferred to the private sector more than a year before the planned completion of the external financing of the project. The effect of this, when the financing could not be completed, was that the assets could be recovered by the Department only with the added encumbrance of the private sector debts which had been raised by LCR. If a department proposes to depart from the normal practice in Public Private Partnerships of transferring assets only when all finance has been raised, then it needs to think through its approach to managing the increased risks it thereby incurs.

Lessons for departments from the restructuring of the deal:

Monitor retained risks from the start of the project

6 The existence of a direct agreement may have made LCR's banks less likely to scrutinise the finances of the project both before and after the contract was signed. For the period that such a risk is retained, departments should, in conjunction with all private sector participants in the deal, ensure that robust project monitoring arrangements are put in place.

Reallocate risks if necessary

7 In procuring a PFI deal, risks should be allocated to the parties best able to manage them. If circumstances change, however, departments should not hesitate to seek a reallocation of risk which will preserve or enhance value for money. In the original deal, the Department considered that the risks attached to raising finance for and building the Link, along with the business risks associated with running an international train service, would be handled better in the private sector. These different risks were bundled together and handed to a single private sector partner. In restructuring the deal, the Department quickly realised that risks had to be reallocated if the Link was to be built. The outcome was a deal that is in many respects more robust than the original.

executive summary

If a project requires public funding, give careful consideration to the most cost-effective route

8 LCR could not have raised all the finance it needed without Government help. However, the use of bonds carrying a Government guarantee rather than a voted loan from the Department to fund the Link, cost the project an additional £80 million. The use of such bonds reflected the unique circumstances of this deal and, in particular, achieved the Government's aim of keeping the project off the public balance sheet. Departments will need to consider this cost-benefit balance with great care if similar situations arise in the future.

If a deal goes wrong, private sector partners should bear their share of the risk

9 Under the PFI, the private sector is paid for taking risk. Responsibility should therefore remain with the private sector should these risks actually occur. In the restructured deal, LCR's shareholders have retained an economic interest in the project while avoiding the full financial consequences of its near collapse. For the future, departments should ensure that equity risk in PFI deals is real and that over-optimism in bidding for contracts will lead to losses if things go wrong.

Specific points for the Department:

The Department should continue to monitor the deal

10 Under the terms of the restructured deal, the taxpayer remains exposed to the financial consequences of Eurostar UK under-performing against forecast passenger volumes but, on the other hand, the taxpayer is entitled to significant dividends if the business is successful. The Department is monitoring progress and has appointed a director to the board of LCR, Eurostar UK's owners. In view of the very long-term nature of these contingent liabilities and assets, the Department should ensure that such active monitoring remains in place and is adequately resourced.

Innovation in quantifying regeneration benefits should be shared with others

11 By attaching a monetary value to the expected regeneration benefits from the Link, the economic appraisal of this deal involved a radical innovation in previously accepted practice. The monetary valuation of expected regeneration benefits from transport and other projects will always be problematical. Nevertheless, the Department rightly intends to share the insights gained in this project with other public bodies to ensure consistency in approach.

The Department should do what it can to ensure that the expected benefits of the Link are realised

12 If regeneration and passenger benefits are not as high as expected, the Link is unlikely to be good value for the taxpayer on economic grounds. To inform future decision making, it is essential therefore that the Department should do what it can to ensure that such benefits are realised. This should include close monitoring and evaluation of the actual value of the regeneration benefits achieved by the Link against those expected when the deal was restructured.

Part 1

This part of the report examines the reasons why the Department chose to restructure the deal for the Link when the original deal with LCR came close to collapse in January 1998. The cause of that near collapse was disappointing performance by the Eurostar UK business. Options considered by the Department included abandoning the project, putting in additional direct grants as LCR had requested and a restructuring. The Department chose the latter option as being one which offered the prospect of completing the Link without undue delay. The restructured deal which followed is in many respects more robust than the original. Section 1 of the Link is under construction and will be purchased on completion by Railtrack. LCR is required to construct Section 2 and Railtrack has an incentive to purchase it, but has not yet exercised its option to do so.

Poorer than expected performance of Eurostar UK put the original deal at risk

1.1 LCR won the Department's competition to build the Link and operate Eurostar UK under a 999 year concession because its bid required the lowest level of direct grants and, in the Department's view, had a more favourable distribution of risk than proposed by the other shortlisted bidder for the project, Eurorail CTRL Ltd. LCR's shareholders are listed in **Figure 1**. The amount of direct grants included in LCR's bid was related to its forecast of Eurostar UK revenues, which were higher than its competitor. When actual Eurostar UK revenues grew considerably less rapidly than forecast, the project was no longer seen as a good investment by private sector investors and LCR realised that it could no longer raise the finance needed to construct the Link and operate Eurostar UK.

1 Shareholders in LCR as at August 1996	
Members	**Percentage shareholding**
Bechtel Limited	19
SG Warburg & Company Limited	19
Virgin Group Limited	18
National Express Group Plc	17.5
Société Nationale des Chemins de Fer Français (SNCF)	8.5
London Electricity Plc	8.5
Ove Arup & Partners	3.5
Sir William Halcrow & Partners Limited	3
Systra Sofuetu Sofrerail	3

Source: The Department

The original deal combined construction of the Link with the privatisation of Eurostar UK

1.2 The deal with LCR was more than just a very large privately financed infrastructure project, it also involved the privatisation of two Government-owned companies (**Figure 2**):

■ Union Railways Limited (URL), responsible for the planning and design of the Link; and

■ European Passenger Services Limited (now Eurostar (UK) Limited or Eurostar UK), the operator of the UK part of the Eurostar international train service. Assets transferred to the private sector on privatisation included the international rail terminal at Waterloo in London and eleven Eurostar train sets. Another seven train sets had previously been sold and leased back by the company.

The deal also included the transfer to LCR of various land and buildings at King's Cross, Stratford and elsewhere in London and Kent. Further information on the Link is at Appendix 3.

2 | **The original contractual structure of the deal**

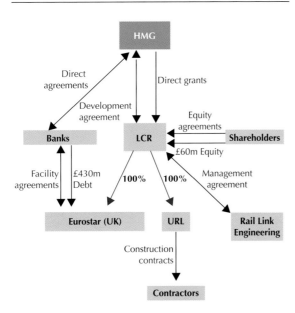

Note: Rail Link Engineering (RLE), is an unincorporated association comprising Bechtel Limited, Ove Arup & Partners, Sir William Halcrow & Partners Limited and Systra Sofuetu Sofrerail. RLE has been contracted to design and project manage Section 1 of the Link.

Source: LCR

1.3 The Department privatised European Passenger Services Limited for policy and commercial reasons. On policy grounds, the privatisation was compatible with the Government's plans to privatise British Rail. The commercial reasons for the privatisation stemmed from the view that Eurostar UK would generate substantial revenues over time. The Department considered that the business was such an attractive proposition that, if transferred free of long-term debt, there would be a lower requirement for public support of the project.

The Department retained the business risk in Eurostar UK

1.4 In 1994, after the pre-qualification round of the competition, the Department informed the bidders that there were two principal criteria for evaluating bids. The contract would be awarded to the bidder that had sought the lowest level of direct grants, provided this was not offset by the amount of risk the bidder wanted the Department to bear.

1.5 At the conclusion of the last round of bidding in December 1995, LCR's bid for direct grants was valued at £1,733 million (**Figure 3**), approximately £400 million less than that sought by Eurorail CTRL Limited. The assessment of the risks that the bidders wanted the Department to bear did not reveal a great disparity between them, although on balance the Department concluded that the terms offered by LCR were more favourable.

1.6 To reduce the risk that the direct grants would be paid too early during the construction of the Link, the Department and LCR agreed that payments would not commence until construction was 68 per cent complete. This precaution, however, did not eliminate the Department's financial risk in the early stages of the project.

3 | **Breakdown of the direct grants to LCR under the original deal**

Grants	Present value of grants (£ millions at 1995 prices)	Dates when payments would have been due
Capital Grant	796	This grant would have been paid in 12 quarterly instalments, the first being £103.96 million and the remaining eleven each being £100 million. The first payment would have been due on the later of either the third anniversary of Financial Close or when construction of the Link was 68 per cent complete.
Deferred Grant	603	This grant would have been paid in four equal quarterly instalments of £270 million. The first payment would have been due 78 months after Financial Close, provided the final permit to use had been issued.
Domestic Capacity	334	This grant would have been paid in 34 equal half-yearly instalments of £26.10 million. The first payment would have been due 78 months after Financial Close, provided the final permit to use had been issued.
TOTAL	**1,733**	

Notes: 1. Financial Close was to have been the later of the date upon which the funding agreements for the second stage of financing were executed or the date the lenders' agent certified to the Department that all conditions precedent to draw down the second stage financing had been complied with or waived.

2. Rebasing the grants to 1997 prices produces a present value of £2,014 million.

3. The Domestic Capacity Charge would have been paid to LCR for providing capacity on the Link for other train operating companies to run services between London and north and east Kent.

Source: The Department

1.7 The Department anticipated that there would be two stages to the winning bidder's financing of the project. The first stage financing would fund the first two years of the project while the winning bidder secured, through a second stage financing, the bulk of the funds it would require to fulfil its obligations. The competition required the bidders to set out the details of their plans for financing the project. LCR adopted the Department's two-stage approach, proposing to raise the second stage finance through the proceeds of a flotation in October 1997 and long-term bank debt. LCR's first stage financing plan comprised £430 million of short- to medium-term bank debt (**Figure 4**) and £60 million of equity from its shareholders. In May 1996, LCR's banks agreed to provide loans for the first stage financing, secured against Eurostar UK.

1.8 As LCR did not have the commercial strength to raise such substantial loans on its own, the Department decided to support the basis on which the loans would be repaid. In a Direct Agreement with LCR's banks the Department agreed that, if the contract with LCR was terminated, the Department would take over and continue operating Eurostar UK as a going concern. In the event of reversion, Eurostar UK would have to service the debt but the Department agreed to pay the operating costs of the business if revenues were insufficient to meet both debt servicing and operating costs. In the unlikely circumstances

4 | Loans for the first stage of financing under the original deal

Bank Loans:	Amounts (£ million)
Commercial Banks Facility[1,2,3]	
United Bank of Switzerland	66 ²/₃
Dai-Icho Kangyo Bank	66 ²/₃
Dresdner Bank (Luxembourg)	66 ²/₃
Citibank	55
Credit Foncier	45
	300
European Investment Bank (EIB)[4,5]	100
Kreditantstalt für Wiederaufbau (KfW)[4,5]	30
TOTAL	**430**

Notes: 1. Bank Facility Agent was the United Bank of Switzerland.

2. The Commercial Banks Facility could be used to fund Eurostar UK operations, for designing and developing the Link and for the purchase of land necessary for its construction.

3. The term of the Commercial Banks Facility was 90 months from 31 May 1996.

4. The EIB and the KfW Facilities could only be used to fund the design and development of the Link and the purchase of land necessary for construction. LCR could not use these funds for Eurostar UK.

5. The term of the EIB and KfW Facilities was 120 months from 31 May 1996.

Source: The Department

5 | Eurostar UK turnover, costs and operational losses

£ million	1998	1999	2000	2001*
Turnover	159	167	187	204
Costs	(257)	(243)	(235)	(248)
Operational Loss (before depreciation)	98	76	48	44

* Budgeted figure

Source: The Department and LCR

(see **Figure 5**) that Eurostar UK's revenues were insufficient to service the outstanding debt, the term over which the debt was to be repaid would be extended. If the deal with LCR was terminated, the Department would therefore get back not just the assets of Eurostar UK but also the liabilities.

The Department was confident that Eurostar UK revenues would grow in line with LCR's forecast

1.9 While there was a risk that Eurostar UK could revert back to public ownership with £430 million of bank debt, the Department considered that the risk was offset by the likely profitability of the business. At the start of the competition to build the Link and before the Eurostar service was operational, transport industry experts expected Eurostar UK to gain a large share of the existing market for travel between London, Paris and Brussels. It was estimated that Eurostar UK would carry over 12.5 million passengers (single journeys) in 1996-97 and that numbers would exceed 15 million journeys by the end of the decade. As LCR had similar expectations for future Eurostar UK patronage, the Department did not challenge the forecasts.

1.10 Nevertheless, the Department foresaw potential risks, particularly because the award of the contract would be well in advance of the second stage financing. If the forecast growth was not achieved, the Department was concerned that LCR or its banks might seek to renegotiate the terms of the deal if a second stage financing could not be completed in the market on acceptable terms. Allaying this concern were three factors:

- SG Warburg & Company Limited, LCR's principal financial adviser, considered that LCR could achieve the second stage financing even if Eurostar UK revenues were 15 per cent lower than forecast;

- in the mid stages of the competition, LCR had the most strongly led and best developed marketing strategies for Eurostar UK; and

■ the Department's view that LCR's shareholders would not risk losing their £60 million equity investment without being confident that second stage financing was achievable.

In the light of lower than expected growth in Eurostar UK revenues the project was not seen as a good investment

1.11 LCR forecast that in 1996-97, Eurostar UK's second full year of operation, 9.5 million passengers would use the train service. The actual number of passengers using the service in that year was 5.1 million (**Figure 6**). As the actual performance of Eurostar UK was significantly lower than that forecast and with expected growth for 1997-98 being less than forecast, LCR realised that the Link would not be viewed as a good investment.

1.12 When the Department was evaluating bids, much depended on the bidders' forecasts. As the evaluation would favour the bidder demanding the lowest level of direct grants there was an in-built incentive to take an optimistic view of future demand for the Eurostar UK service. Although the inclusion of private finance in a project can be seen as a means of tempering undue optimism, at the first stage financing of this project there were two structural features that checked the need for detailed scrutiny of passenger forecasts by investors. The first was the Department's support for debt repayments in the Direct Agreement. Although such support was needed if LCR was to raise debt, it also effectively eliminated the need for the lending banks to satisfy themselves that the project could repay the loan. The second concerned the level of equity invested by LCR's shareholders. LCR's shareholders subscribed £60 million, just over 12 per cent of the total stage 1 finance. This equity comprised £30 million of capitalised tender costs and £30 million in cash. Since all the shareholders were also suppliers to LCR, there is some doubt as to whether the value of the equity at risk was sufficient to balance the shareholders' interest in

becoming major contractors to the project. LCR expected that project development costs amounting to £92 million would be paid to its own shareholders in the period leading up to the planned flotation in October 1997.

1.13 The reliance on optimistic forecasts was not the only factor that undermined LCR's attempts to convince potential investors that the project was a sound investment opportunity. LCR experienced difficulties marketing Eurostar UK to the widest audience of potential passengers. These difficulties stemmed from the operation of the train service being the responsibility of three different companies, each one responsible for the service within the national boundaries of the three countries served by the business. SNCF and SNCB, the State-owned companies responsible for domestic rail services in France and Belgium respectively, are the two other companies that run the Eurostar international train service. Eurostar UK, by contrast a private company whose sole business is the operation of the UK arm of the international passenger train service, experienced difficulties convincing SNCF and SNCB to adopt vigorous and co-ordinated marketing strategies.

1.14 Eurostar UK also encountered competition that LCR and the Department did not foresee. All the forecasts anticipated that demand on the London to Paris route would continue to grow at historic rates and that Eurostar UK would draw a considerable number of passengers from the airlines. The rate of growth in demand for Eurostar UK has slowed considerably because the growth of low-cost airlines, competing on cost but also offering more choice of destinations, has drawn leisure travellers away from the traditional London to Paris route. Moreover, the adverse impact of low cost airlines has gone beyond suppressing growth in passenger numbers, it has also restricted the ability of Eurostar UK to increase fares for leisure travellers.

1.15 The Channel Tunnel fire in November 1996, just over five months after LCR took over Eurostar UK severely disrupted Eurostar services for two months and continued to impact upon the efficiency of the service for a further five months. The Department considered that the fire would delay LCR's proposed flotation by the amount of time needed for passenger demand to pick up, following the resumption of full operations.

The original deal came close to collapsing

1.16 In January 1998 LCR publicly approached the Department with a request for £1,200 million[6] of additional direct grant. At this time LCR was at the point

| 6 | **LCR's original forecast of Eurostar UK passenger numbers** |

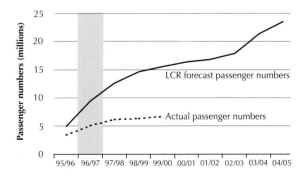

Source: LCR

6   *1995 prices*

of exhausting the funds it had raised through the first stage financing and there was little if any prospect that it would be able to raise further funds from private sector sources.

The Department did not obtain all the information to which it was entitled from LCR

1.17 The Department knew before the award of the contract that revenues from Eurostar UK were crucial to the success of the project. In August 1996, the Department's financial advisers, (J Henry Schroder & Co Ltd and Deloitte and Touche) set out detailed proposals for monitoring LCR's financial health. The Department did not, however, insist that LCR comply fully with its obligations to supply financial information.

1.18 Until the fire in the Channel Tunnel in November 1996, the Department instructed its advisers not to press LCR for information about Eurostar UK revenues. The Department's reasons were:

a) that LCR, having taken over Eurostar UK on 31 May 1996, required time to convert the business culture within the company from a public sector railway operator to a market driven business;

b) that the implementation of LCR's marketing strategies required time to become effective; and

c) that a rigorous analysis of LCR's performance, shortly after it had taken control of Eurostar UK, could have impacted adversely on the contractual relationship.

1.19 The Department's stance contributed to the decision not to implement a proposal, made in August 1996, for an independent review of LCR's revenue projections. When the Department did sanction this work in December 1996, LCR had already commissioned L.E.K. Consulting (LEK), a transport consultancy, to analyse the demand for the Eurostar UK service. The Department therefore decided to await LEK's report before considering what action, if any, needed to be taken.

1.20 The Department did not institute formal and regular finance progress meetings with LCR until April 1997. At the inaugural meeting the Department, after taking advice from its legal advisers (CMS Cameron McKenna), agreed that rather than receive detailed monthly reports on progress towards the second stage financing, it would receive outline reports that LCR would expand upon at subsequent progress meetings. LCR had informed the Department that the second stage financing was still possible but, following the disruption caused by the Channel Tunnel fire, LCR's position would be precarious if the Department insisted on receiving detailed reports and, in compliance with its obligations, forwarded these reports to LCR's bankers. LCR was concerned that its bankers would call in the loans despite the Department's support for repayment of the bank debt in the Direct Agreement. The Department considered that this would have been

likely as only £192 million of the £430 million loans package had been drawn down and the banks would have been able to cap their exposure. By allowing LCR to continue to operate Eurostar UK, extra time was secured to turn the business around. The Department reasoned that with the debt fully drawn down, there would be an incentive on the banks to support a restructuring of the deal which would result in earlier repayments of the outstanding loans than would be likely if they had to depend on revenues from a publicly run Eurostar UK.

The Department wanted LCR to exhaust other avenues of funding before exposing the taxpayer to increased financial risk

1.21 In February 1997 LCR informed the Department that to convince investors of the soundness of the Eurostar UK business following the Channel Tunnel fire there was a need to collect more Eurostar UK revenue data. As a result, LCR had to postpone the flotation from October 1997 to March 1998. This meant that LCR would exhaust its stage 1 finances in January 1998. To bridge this funding gap, LCR proposed to raise finance by selling the eleven Eurostar train sets it still owned and leasing them back from the new owner. LCR's access to these funds was, however, prevented under the contract until after completion of the second stage financing. In May 1997 LCR approached the Department to obtain a relaxation of the contract.

1.22 The request effectively asked the Department to increase its financial risk in the project by £230 million. If Eurostar UK reverted to the public sector, the Department would become liable for the leasing payments. The Department considered that it was the only party being asked to increase its financial exposure, as LCR had not proposed either raising further debt or obtaining a further injection of equity from its shareholders. In July 1997, Ministers met LCR and suggested that LCR should seek additional financial support from its shareholders and lenders. LCR's response was that its shareholders were not prepared to increase their investment and its banks would only lend more if the Government provided additional financial support.

1.23 In August 1997 the Department informed LCR of the detailed terms on which it would be granted access to the leasing proceeds. The Department considered that LCR would find the terms so unfavourable that it would be compelled to go back to its shareholders.

LCR sought an alternative solution before it ran out of money

1.24 While LCR was considering how to bridge the funding gap, it received LEK's report on future passenger demand for the Eurostar UK service. The analysis revealed that demand was strong but at levels lower than those forecast by LCR. Using these figures, Eurostar UK was expected to lose £750 million more in the medium term than LCR had forecast in its bid. The size of this expected loss put the second stage financing beyond LCR's reach and, in September 1997, LCR communicated these findings to the Department.

1.25 LCR submitted a number of options for taking the project forward, including the involvement of Railtrack in the construction and operation of the Link. Each option depended, in one way or another, on the Department increasing the level of direct grants, paying a revenue subsidy, bearing some Eurostar UK revenue risk or guaranteeing a long-dated LCR bond.

1.26 By late 1997, however, LCR had discarded all options that did not include bringing Railtrack into the project. Negotiations with Railtrack commenced, but in January 1998 LCR realised that a deal was unlikely. Close to insolvency, LCR abandoned the negotiations and publicly approached the Department with a request for £1,200 million[6] of additional direct grant.

The Department wanted the Link completed without a material increase in the direct grants

1.27 Immediately following LCR's announcement in September 1997 that second stage financing could not be reached, the Department considered its options and instructed its advisers to scrutinise LEK's forecasts for Eurostar UK. The advisers considered that LEK's projections of revenue and demand appeared to lie towards the top end of the plausible range. In January 1998, the Department commissioned Booze-Allen & Hamilton to provide an independent review of the forecasts. In April 1998, the Department was provided with two new scenarios for future Eurostar UK revenues, a central case and a downside case. These scenarios are detailed in **Figure 7**.

1.28 The Department seriously considered abandoning the project and taking the Eurostar UK business, along with the intellectual and other assets of LCR, back into the public sector. However, the option of terminating the contract with LCR and abandoning or retendering the project was rejected. The Government wanted the Link built and the Department considered that a new contract would take two years to negotiate and so prolong property blight, that Railtrack's likely participation would deter others from entering a competition and those that did would seek a significant price premium to avoid the difficulties experienced by LCR.

1.29 In the Department's view, the best deal would be won through restructuring the existing deal with LCR. The Department was aware of this as early as November 1997, but decided to wait until the LCR

Board publicly announced that the company was in difficulty before taking the initiative. The Department rejected LCR's request for additional direct grants, but, in accordance with the contract, granted LCR a cure period of 30 days to find an acceptable solution. The objectives the Department set LCR for such a solution included:

■ the construction of the entire Link;

■ the injection of new private sector management into Eurostar UK;

■ the commitment of third parties with the financial strength to meet their obligations; and

---

| 7 | Summary of forecast increases in passenger numbers and revenues per passenger assumed under the four scenarios |

	LCR (% annual increases)			
	Management Case		Downside Case	
	Passengers	Yield	Passengers	Yield
Section 1	7	4.9	5.6	2.45
Section 2	7.5	4.9	5	2.45

	Government (% annual increases)			
	Central Case		Downside Case	
	Passengers	Yield	Passengers	Yield
Section 1	6.7	1.4	5.7	1
Section 2	11	2.5	9.7	3

Notes: There were four main forecasts of Eurostar UK patronage. Two forecasts were prepared for LCR, and two were prepared by the Government's advisers, Booze-Allen & Hamilton. The forecasts provided estimated passenger numbers and revenues per passenger (known as Yields):

The LCR Management Case: This was LCR's view of the most likely level of demand and revenues. It assumed there would be an increase in passenger numbers of seven per cent on the opening of Section 1, 7.5 per cent on completion of the Link and that there would be an uplift of 4.9 per cent in revenue per passenger at the opening of each Section.

The LCR Downside Case: This assumed lower passenger and revenue uplifts and represented LCR's pessimistic scenario. It assumed a 5.6 per cent uplift in passenger numbers at Section 1 opening, a further five per cent uplift on completion of the Link and that revenue per passenger would increase by 2.45 per cent at the opening of each Section.

The Government Central Case: This was the forecast of expected passenger numbers and yields per passenger that formed the basis of the value for money assessment of the project. As Booze-Allen & Hamilton considered that LCR's forecasts were optimistic, the Government Central Case used lower estimates of passengers and, in particular, revenue per passenger. The Central Case assumed a 6.7 per cent increase in passenger numbers for Section 1 and 11 per cent for Section 2. The increases in revenues per passenger, however, were much lower at 1.4 per cent for Section 1 and 2.5 per cent on completion of the Link.

The Government Downside Case: This was the pessimistic scenario. It assumed a 5.7 per cent increase in passengers for Section 1 and a 9.7 per cent increase on completion. The increases in revenue per passenger were one per cent for Section 1 and three per cent on completion.

Source: LCR

■ the achievement of a true Public Private Partnership with each risk allocated to the party best able to manage it and with rewards commensurate with the risks.

Apart from the principal participants in the project, the restructuring also involved a large number of professional advisers. The key advisers are listed at Appendix 4.

1.30 In February 1998 LCR submitted the framework of a solution that was seen as providing the basis for meeting these objectives. This won LCR an extension of the cure period so that details of changes to the contract could be considered. To keep LCR solvent during this period, the Department agreed the sale and lease back of Eurostar train sets, but with proceeds paid into an account over which the Department and LCR had joint control. As a result, the Department acquired powers to scrutinise LCR's outgoings. The Department also won concessions from Bechtel Limited, SG Warburg & Company Limited and Railtrack. The two shareholders in LCR agreed to defer charges for their work and Railtrack agreed to defer existing Eurostar UK track access charges until the conclusion of the restructured deal. These charges were at risk if the negotiations broke down and the contract terminated.

1.31 The basis of a restructured deal acceptable to the Government was reached in June 1998. The agreed principles were that:

■ there would be no material increase in the amount of direct grants for the project;

■ construction of the Link would be split into two sections;

■ the construction risk and the revenue risk from the ownership of the Eurostar UK business would be split and re-allocated;

■ there would be additional public support in the form of guarantees and direct loans; and

■ the length of the concession would be reduced from 999 years to 90 years, ending in 2086.

1.32 After receiving LCR's final proposals the Department undertook a benchmarking exercise to ascertain whether the restructured deal offered value for money. The Department compared the restructured deal with its own assessment of a retendered deal. The Department considered that a new competition could have yielded savings of up to £200 million. Such savings were, however, based on the assumption that other bidders would be interested in competing against Railtrack, something the Department considered was unlikely.

The restructured deal is in many respects more robust than the original

1.33 During the autumn of 1998 LCR awarded contracts for the construction of Section 1 of the Link. While the Department accepted an increase in long-term financial risks for the taxpayer, many short-term risks remain with the private sector. In some cases these risks have been spread beyond LCR to companies considered capable of bearing the risks.

Financing the construction of Section 1 of the Link is no longer dependent on the performance of Eurostar UK

1.34 LCR failed to convince investors that the project was a worthwhile investment opportunity because Eurostar UK did not generate the required revenue. The restructured deal is no longer dependent on such a project finance approach. Instead the project will be financed by debt that will not be at risk from the financial performance of Eurostar UK. During discussions, Railtrack informed the Department that it could not commit to purchase the entire Link until the outcome of the Rail Regulator's access charge review for the domestic network was known. The restructured deal therefore divided the construction of the Link into two sections. The Government has guaranteed bonds issued by LCR and Railtrack agreed to provide guarantees that will allow LCR to borrow up to £700 million of commercial debt, during the construction of Section 1.

Construction risk remains in the private sector

1.35 As the principal risk taker for the construction, in terms of both cost and time, Railtrack has acquired effective control over an LCR subsidiary company, Union Railways (South), that is responsible for constructing Section 1 of the Link and owns all the relevant assets. Railtrack has agreed to purchase Section 1 from Union Railways (South) for the actual cost of construction plus financing costs, less the direct grants paid by the Department to LCR.

1.36 Railtrack's rate of return for Section 1 of the Link depends on a number of factors, but was set to be broadly comparable to the rate of return of 7.5 per cent[7] allowed on the regulated network at the time the deal was restructured. A construction cost overrun would result in a higher purchase price, reducing Railtrack's rate of return. A cost underrun would improve the return.

part one

---

7   Railtrack's Access Charges for Franchised Passenger Services: The Future Level of Charges (Office of the Rail Regulator, January 1995)

8   **The distribution of savings if the actual construction costs of Section 1 of the Link are less than the target construction cost**

	Share of Savings (per cent)	
	Savings up to £239 million	Savings above £239 million
Railtrack	40	50
Rail Link Engineering	40	-
The Department	20	50

Source: The Department

9   **Shareholdings in ICRR**

Members	Percentage shareholding
National Express Group*	40
SNCF*	35
SNCB	15
British Airways	10
TOTAL	**100**

* NEG and SNCF are also shareholders in LCR

Source: The Department

10   **ICRR's reduction of revenue risk by reducing operating costs**

This figure shows that ICRR has reduced the addressable costs of operating Eurostar UK by £19 million in 1999 and £23 million in 2000 compared with the operating costs incurred in 1998.

	1998 £m	1999 £m	2000 £m
Total costs	257	243	235
Less:			
Eurotunnel usage charges	80	83	81
Railtrack access charges	39	40	36
Redundancy	-	-	1
Distribution and sales	20	21	22
Addressable costs	118	99	95
Cost reductions achieved	-	19	23
Cost reductions forecast in ICRR bid	-	*10*	*11*

Source: LCR and ICRR

1.37 Concerned that the target construction cost could be too high and that savings against this figure would enhance Railtrack's rate of return, the Department negotiated a right to a share of any such savings (see **Figure 8**).

The restructured deal contains improved arrangements for sharing and managing Eurostar UK revenue risk

1.38 The track access charges payable to Railtrack by Eurostar UK between 2003 and 2010 are subject to a revenue sharing agreement. If Eurostar UK's revenues are greater than forecast in the LCR Management Case, the charges it will pay to Railtrack will be increased. If Eurostar UK's revenues fall short of the LCR Management Case, the charges will be reduced. The amount of revenue sharing is subject to a cap and collar and is on a sliding scale, differing according to whether Railtrack exercises its option to purchase Section 2 of the Link.

1.39 Under its licence, Railtrack is prohibited from operating train services and so could not take over the operation of Eurostar UK. This limitation compelled LCR to separate the Eurostar UK business from the construction and operation of the Link. This separation aligned with the Department's objective that Eurostar UK should be operated under new management arrangements. LCR's solution was to appoint a separate train operating company. In 1999, at the conclusion of a competition between ICRR and Virgin Group Limited, the former was appointed to operate and manage Eurostar UK, which will remain under the ownership of LCR. ICRR's shareholders are listed at **Figure 9**.

1.40 ICRR agreed to operate and manage Eurostar UK until 31 December 2010 in return for a management fee of two per cent of turnover, equating to some £3.7 million in 2000. There is also a risk sharing mechanism based upon an operating cashflow bid by ICRR. This is distinct from revenue risk because ICRR can mitigate revenue shortfalls by cutting costs, something it achieved in 1999 and 2000 (see **Figure 10**). If Eurostar UK cashflow runs below ICRR's bid line, ICRR must share the downside risk with LCR. Payments by ICRR to LCR are capped at £100 million over the life of the contract and limited to a maximum of £20 million in any one year, subject to any payment obligation greater than £20 million being carried over to the following year. In 2000, Eurostar UK cashflow was below the bid line to the extent that ICRR had to pay £2.1 million to LCR. There is also a sharing of the upside, capped at £250 million over the life of the contract. Nevertheless, while LCR has transferred revenue risk to other parties, the majority of the risk has been retained (see Figure 5).

The Department has improved its monitoring of the project

1.41 The Department has ensured that the involvement of new parties, such as ICRR and Railtrack, has not diluted its ability to influence and monitor the project. The Department has a special share in ICRR entitling it to a fixed dividend and certain information. In the ICRR management agreement, the Department has also protected its right to take Eurostar UK back into public ownership in the event of default under the Development Agreement with LCR. The Department is a co-signatory to the contract that governs Railtrack's participation in the project. In the restructured deal with LCR, the Department obtained and has exercised the right to appoint a director to the board of the company and has included more explicit terms setting out the information that it considers necessary to monitor not only progress but also the financial health of the project.

1.42 In tandem with its increased powers the Department is more actively monitoring the performance of LCR and others. The Department's advisers are now receiving the information they consider essential to assess and update the Department's retained risks. In March 2000 the Department commissioned Booze-Allen & Hamilton to review Eurostar UK passenger and revenue forecasts, following LCR's assessment that Eurostar UK performance will fall below the Government's downside case for the year 2000.

Financing for Section 2 of the Link is still to be secured

1.43 The restructured deal has secured the continued private sector operation of Eurostar UK and is likely to realise the completion of Section 1 of the Link during 2003. While LCR has a contractual obligation to construct the entire Link it does not, at present, have the financial backing from the private sector to ensure construction of Section 2.

1.44 LCR has access to considerable funds; these include the staged payments of direct grants to be paid by the Department, a right to issue further Government-guaranteed bonds and the purchase proceeds from Railtrack for Section 1 of the Link. These sums, however, are not sufficient to finance the construction of Section 2 and projected Eurostar UK losses. To ensure that there is the finance to satisfy its obligations, LCR must raise approximately £600 million of commercial debt, although the exact amount will depend on LCR's cash position at the time.

1.45 While LCR had to raise commercial debt to fund the construction of Section 1 it was able to do so because Railtrack guaranteed the debt. Similar support for Section 2 is not assured. Railtrack has not committed itself to purchasing Section 2, but does have an option to do so which it can exercise at any time up to July 2003. There are, however, a number of incentives for Railtrack to commit support to Section 2, including:

- an upward adjustment of the access charges payable, giving it a greater rate of return;

- a right to purchase a share of profits from the development of land at King's Cross and Stratford.

1.46 Railtrack has undertaken a due diligence examination of Section 2, with a view to establishing whether and on what terms it would be willing to exercise its option in 2001. The results have been shared with the Department and LCR and discussions between the parties are continuing. If Railtrack does not exercise its option to purchase Section 2, LCR will need to examine how it can raise all the funds needed to ensure completion of the Link. Until Railtrack's option expires in July 2003 or is surrendered earlier, LCR cannot sell Section 2 to any other organisation.

Part 2

The complex financing of the
Link requires long-term
Government support

This part of the report examines the implications for public expenditure of the arrangements agreed between the Government and the private sector to ensure that the funds required to build the Link would be raised. Although the taxpayer is now exposed to considerable financial risk if Eurostar UK does not perform as well as expected, the Department has taken steps to share in any long-term profits if the business is successful.

The Link will be financed from a complex mixture of public and private finance and guarantees

2.1 Under the terms of the original deal, LCR had planned to raise finance from private sector investors in two tranches:

a) "Financial Close 1" in May 1996 raised £430 million of debt and £60 million of equity for the design and enabling works of the Link, LCR head office costs and Eurostar UK losses up to "Financial Close 2";

b) "Financial Close 2" would have raised a further £1,000 million of equity and £3,000-£4,000 million of debt to repay the existing debt, fund construction of the entire Link and to make good any continuing Eurostar UK losses.

2.2 LCR's inability to complete the second stage of financing and the terms on which the project was restructured meant that these arrangements had to be amended. With the split of construction into two sections and Railtrack's option over Section 2 raising uncertainty about the amount and timing of finance required, it was agreed that "Financial Close 2" should only raise funds for the construction of Section 1. A third tranche of funds (Financial Close 3) would be raised at a later date to fund construction of Section 2 of the Link. However, as a result of the delay to "Financial Close 2", short-term funding would be required if LCR was to remain solvent during negotiations on the shape of a restructured deal. This was achieved by the sale-and-leaseback of eleven Eurostar trainsets, backed by a Government guarantee that LCR's obligations to make

lease payments would be fulfilled until the sale-and-leaseback could be terminated when full funding became available.

2.3 In the restructured deal with LCR, the longer term funding of the Link and continued support for Eurostar UK operations depended on the Government's agreement to provide guarantees, pay grants to subsidise construction and operation of the Link and to lend money directly to LCR. Railtrack was also a key participant but LCR shareholders' entitlement to future dividends has been curtailed. In view of the complexity of the financing for this project, we commissioned RBC Dominion Securities (a part of the Royal Bank of Canada Group) to review a number of key areas on our behalf. The findings of this review are set out in full at Appendix 5 with references, as appropriate, in this part of the report.

LCR could only issue bonds to investors on the back of a Government guarantee

2.4 In the Department's view, the problems surrounding the refinancing of the Channel Tunnel had made large infrastructure projects unappealing to investors and there was a perception, which is wrong but still exists, that the Tunnel and the Link are one and the same project. Against this background and the uncertainty over the future performance of Eurostar UK, LCR considered that it would be impossible to raise fresh equity to allow construction of the Link to begin in October 1998. The alternative of raising finance entirely from bank debt was highly unlikely for a number of reasons. First, a syndicated loan of as much as £4,000 million would have been unprecedented in the debt markets. Second, a financing structure involving only debt would have been unacceptable to lending banks, as LCR's ratio of debt to equity would have been too high. Third, assuming such a large amount could have been raised, LCR considered that investors would demand very high levels of interest to compensate them for the risks involved.

2.5 The cost of finance was important because the level of interest paid on borrowing had been a significant factor in LCR's response to the Government's position that the Link should be built without any material increase in the level of grants agreed for the original deal. To achieve this, LCR had assumed bond financing with a Government guarantee to investors that they would be paid interest and that their capital would be repaid. Such a guarantee would enable LCR to approach the market with certainty that funds would be raised and at much lower interest rates than would otherwise be the case. The Department agreed with LCR that assistance would be needed in raising finance and, following intensive negotiations, the Government provided a guarantee of the payment of interest and repayment of principal on up to £3,750 million of LCR bonds to help finance both sections of the Link. Financial Close 2 took place in February 1999, following the issue by LCR of an initial tranche of £2,650 million of bonds guaranteed by the Government (**Figure 11**).

11 **To fund Section 1 of the Link and Eurostar UK, LCR issued bonds backed by a Government guarantee**

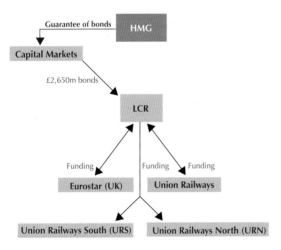

Source: The Department

2.6 The issue of fixed interest long-term bonds to finance a construction project is somewhat unusual. Given the potential for variations in the timing and amount of cash required in a construction project, the flexibility to draw down loans as and when needed can help to reduce the cost of funding. We therefore asked RBC Dominion Securities to examine the availability and cost of funds in the financial markets in late 1998 and early 1999 and to compare this with the terms obtained by LCR in the bond markets. The conclusion is that the bonds represented good value in terms of the interest paid compared with what was available in the markets at the time. Furthermore, there are material doubts as to whether it would have been possible to raise all the financing required from the loan market (Appendix 5, paragraphs 1-20).

Railtrack has agreed to buy Section 1 and has guaranteed part of LCR's borrowing

2.7 Railtrack will purchase Section 1 of the Link following its construction. The price, net of Government grants received by LCR, is to be based on the actual cost of building Section 1 and will include an interest element to compensate LCR for the cost of funding construction. Interest is calculated at a fixed rate of seven per cent a year up to the agreed target construction cost and LIBOR[8] thereafter. It is expected that the purchase price for Section 1, including accrued interest but after the deduction of direct grants, will be some £1,500 million.

2.8 In addition to issuing Government-guaranteed bonds (GGBs), LCR put in place facilities to draw, if needed, up to £700 million of debt from a consortium of commercial banks and other sources. If used, LCR's obligations to service and repay the debt have been guaranteed by Railtrack on the condition that the money can only be used for the design, development and construction of Section 1. Some £500 million of the debt facilities will mature on or before September 2005, while the remainder is expected to be assumed by Railtrack (**Figure 12**).

12 **Railtrack will purchase Section 1 and has guaranteed part of LCR's borrowings**

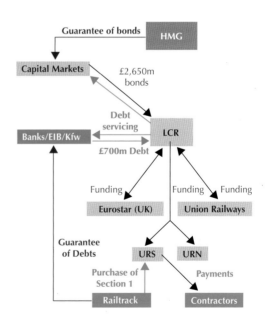

Source: The Department

8   *London Inter-Bank Offered Rate - the rate of interest offered on loans between first-class banks for a specified period (usually three to six months)*

In addition to grants and guarantees of access charges, the Government has agreed to lend money to LCR directly

2.9 Government grants of £2,014 million for the construction and operating costs of the entire Link have been agreed. Capital Grants of £1,619 million are payable on the achievement of set construction milestones. In addition, Domestic Capacity Charges totalling £395 million will be made to secure capacity on the Link for domestic passenger trains for a period of 17 years. These grants are expected to be reduced by land rental payments to the Government from 2030 worth some £266 million. Such land rentals are, however, dependent on the ability of Eurostar UK to generate sufficient passenger income to meet them.

2.10 Like domestic train operators, Eurostar UK currently pays access charges to Railtrack for use of the existing track from the Channel Tunnel to Waterloo. Moreover, Eurostar UK also has to pay usage charges to Eurotunnel. Until 2006, the usage charges are payable irrespective of the actual use made of the Tunnel. This means that, until passenger numbers exceed between 10 and 12 million a year, Eurostar UK will continue to pay a minimum charge to Eurotunnel. Such charges, which at present constitute some 35 per cent of Eurostar UK operating costs, have been guaranteed by the Government since the opening of the Tunnel.

2.11 Eurostar UK will be required to pay access charges to Railtrack for the use of the new track and stations. These access charges are designed to recover operating costs and to provide Railtrack with a rate of return on the target construction cost of the Link, taking into account the Government grants received, the ongoing cost of servicing borrowings and expected revenue from domestic train operators using the Link. Access charges, and as a consequence the rate of return, will be higher if Railtrack opts to build both Sections of the Link and are also subject to variations in Eurostar UK revenues between 2003 and 2010.

2.12 To give Railtrack an assurance that it will receive a minimum income stream on its investment, the structure of the deal also involves separate arrangements whereby the Government has guaranteed access charges payable by Eurostar UK to Railtrack for a period of 50 years from the scheduled opening of Section 1 in 2003. If, for example, Eurostar UK becomes permanently unable to pay access charges, the Government will have to pay. In addition, the Government will make top-up payments if the International Rail Regulator reduces the level of access charges paid by Eurostar UK. In the event that Eurostar UK is unable to pay access charges, the guarantee would be fulfilled in practice by the Department lending LCR additional money through an access charge loan facility (**Figure 13**).

---

13 The Government will pay grants and has guaranteed access charge payments made by Eurostar UK to Railtrack

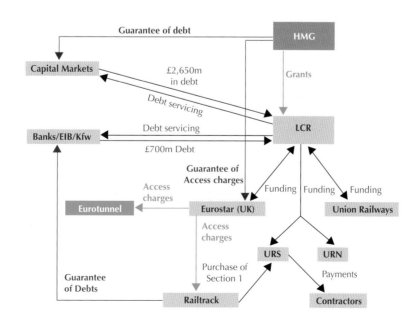

Source: The Department

LCR's original shareholders have not provided new equity finance but retain an economic interest in the project

2.13 One of the Department's objectives for the restructuring of the deal was to remove the existing shareholders from management control but require them to maintain an economic interest in the success of the project. The original shareholders with a continued fixed interest in LCR have converted 95 per cent of their equity stake into preference shares. The preference shares accrue interest at 7 per cent a year from February 1999 (Financial Close 2) and will be repaid 50 per cent on completion of Section 1 (the scheduled repayment for this stage will be £37million, including the rolled up interest) and 50 per cent on completion of Section 2. The remaining 5 per cent of their original investment will remain at risk as ordinary shares. LCR's original shareholders did not therefore lose their original investment and did not contribute any further equity to the project (**Figure 14**).

2.14 As the shareholders stood to receive different financial benefits from the restructured business, it was considered that they would need an incentive to approve the restructuring. It was therefore intended that the original shareholders would convert their entire equity to preference shares and new ordinary shareholders would be brought in. However, new shareholders would have required an incentive to purchase shares in LCR, given the uncertainty of receiving dividends in the near future. It was proposed that the new shareholders should be allowed to purchase the considerable tax losses that had built up in

LCR since 1996 at a reduced price in order to provide a return in the short term. However, prospective investors would not buy LCR shares without an assurance that such tax losses could be bought and used elsewhere. Such an assurance was refused by the Inland Revenue on general taxation policy grounds.

2.15 Some of the original shareholders and their associated businesses have made and may make further profits through alternative routes. For instance, Bechtel will receive 40 per cent of any savings on the target construction cost for Section 1, up to a maximum specified level. Bechtel will also take a share of what the Department's advisers considered were higher than normal project management fees charged by Rail Link Engineering and agreed during wide-reaching negotiations on the restructured deal. SBC Warburg Dillon Read was joint corporate finance adviser with Deutsche Bank to LCR, joint lead bookrunner on the sale of the GGBs and the joint arranger with Deutsche Bank of swaps for the LCR interest rate hedging strategy.

The decision to use Government-guaranteed bonds was finely balanced

2.16 In considering how the Government could assist LCR to raise debt finance, the Department had to take a number of key decisions on the type of debt that would provide the best value for the taxpayer and how best to go about raising the large sums required.

---

14   **LCR shareholders did not provide new equity but retain an interest in the project**

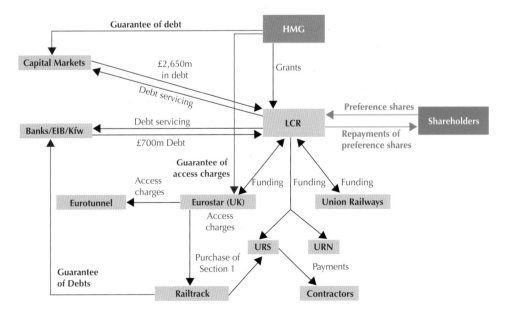

Source: The Department

Government-guaranteed bonds, issued by LCR, were seen as having advantages over gilts

2.17 The key question for the Department was whether it would be better value to fund the Link through a voted loan to LCR (funded ultimately through general Gilt issuance) or through an issue of corporate bonds by LCR, backed by a Government guarantee but not involving additional public borrowing. The Department considered that a guarantee was justified because:

a) the concept of the Link as a flagship Public Private Partnership would be maintained as there would still be private money and private sector disciplines in the project;

b) the use of gilts would risk signalling to other bidders for Public Private Partnership projects the Government's readiness to assume financing risk; and

c) the guarantee would keep the project off the public sector balance sheet, thereby avoiding any risk that direct public funding would contribute to a potential breach of international obligations concerning the UK debt to gross domestic product ratio or lead to adverse market perceptions of the management of the UK economy.

2.18 Unlike an additional issue of Gilts, the GGBs would not be classified as public borrowing if there was a very low likelihood that the guarantee would ever be called. Following consultations with the Office for National Statistics, the Government guarantee of LCR bonds was classified as a contingent liability rather than borrowing. This decision was based on the fact that, given the independent Eurostar UK forecasts provided by Booze-Allen & Hamilton, there was no reasonable operating scenario in which the guarantee of LCR's bonds would be called, provided the access charge loan facility was made available to LCR when required.

These advantages were secured at a cost of some £80 million

2.19 The GGBs for Section 1 of the Link were issued in three tranches during February 1999 at interest rate margins of between 0.28 and 0.37 of a percentage point above the Government's cost of borrowing in the Gilt market and maturing in 2010 (£1,000 million), 2028 (£1,275 million) and 2038 (£375 million). At fixed rates of interest of 4.5 and 4.75 per cent, these margins implied an extra funding cost of around £80 million over comparable Gilts, even though the risk for investors is identical. The reasons for this apparent disparity are set out in detail by RBC Dominion Securities in Appendix 5 (paragraphs 40-62). In summary, there were two key factors which led bond investors to demand a premium over comparable Gilts:

a) The GGBs at each maturity were small in comparison with Gilts, so there would be fewer opportunities to buy and sell what were regarded as Eurobonds by investors at a fair price in the secondary market for such securities. This relative illiquidity meant that investors would demand a higher rate of interest on the bonds than on Gilts;

b) Despite their relatively small size in comparison with Gilts, the GGBs represented large issues in their own right in the Eurobond market. As a consequence, a further interest rate premium would be required if the entire issue was to be sold to Eurobond investors.

The extra cost of funding through Government - guaranteed bonds was controlled through careful handling of the market

2.20 In June 1998, when the agreement to provide a Government guarantee for the bonds was given, conditions in the sterling capital markets were relatively stable and it was expected that the bonds could be issued at a relatively small interest premium to Gilts. Before any GGBs could be issued, their detailed terms had to be agreed and the restructured deal itself, including the use of GGBs, needed to be reviewed by the European Commission for compatibility with state aid provisions. In late 1998 and early 1999, however, financial instability caused by the Russian debt crisis and the near failure of a major hedge fund caused interest rate margins on corporate bonds to increase dramatically against the rates payable on "risk free" Gilts. To get the best deal on the GGBs issued by LCR, the issue had to be managed carefully in the run-up to the sale and the GGBs themselves had to be made to appear as Gilt like as possible.

2.21 The method used to price and distribute the GGBs was decided in consultation with the market. Three ways of issuing the GGBs were considered:

a) a straightforward auction through the UK Debt Management Office (lowest issuing costs but giving least control of the prices at which the GGBs would be sold);

b) a bookbuilding process in which a lead manager would invite bids at various prices to assess the strength of demand (possibly higher issuing costs than an auction but more certainty that all of the GGBs would be sold at managed prices);

c) an underwritten issue where one or more banks agree to buy any GGBs that remain unsold (the most expensive option although demand risk is fully transferred to the underwriters).

2.22 Early advice had indicated that an auction process would be acceptable to the market, provided the GGBs were made as Gilt like as possible. Two key conditions were required: that the GGBs would be accepted by the FTSE Bond Index Committee for inclusion in its Gilt Index and that the Bank of England should accept the GGBs as eligible for its market security operations. The FTSE Bond Index Committee rejected the inclusion of the GGBs as they were not Gilts. The Bank of England indicated that, consistent with its treatment of new types of financial instrument, it was unwilling to include the GGBs as eligible in market security operations until their liquidity had been proven through successful trading in the market.

2.23 As a result, investors did not favour an auction and expressed a strong preference that the GGBs should be issued as Eurobonds, either as a bookbuilt or underwritten offer. The Department, in consultation with its financial adviser, the Treasury and the Debt Management Office, opted for book building on the grounds of cost. Following a competition supervised by the Department and its financial adviser, SBC Warburg Dillon Read and HSBC were appointed by LCR as lead managers for the book building. At under half the cost of an underwritten offer, their fees were reasonable, given the large size of the issues, reputational risk and the need to support the GGBs in the after market if required.

2.24 Action was taken to make the GGBs attractive to the market. For example, to appeal to as wide a variety of investors as possible, the interest payment dates on the GGBs coincided with those on comparable Gilts maturing at similar dates. The GGBs were issued around the time that the Gilt markets were at their most favourable for the 12 months around February 1999. The interest rate margins over Gilts on the GGBs were lower than comparable AAA rated issues and the GGBs have generally performed well since their launch in comparison with those issues. Our overall conclusion is that the marketing and launch of the GGBs was a success (Appendix 5, paragraphs 55-98 set out the detail). In the longer term, this was also important in creating positive perceptions amongst investors ahead of any further bond issues by LCR for Section 2 of the Link.

The taxpayer faces both open-ended financial risks and the possibility of returns

2.25 Although funding for construction of Section 1 of the Link was assured, the Department had to consider how continuing uncertainty over the future performance of Eurostar UK and the financial health of LCR should be addressed. In doing so the Department aimed to avoid any adverse impact on the completion of the Link while ensuring that the Government guarantee of LCR's bonds would be highly unlikely to be called.

Large amounts of public money will be lent directly to LCR if Eurostar UK continues to underperform

2.26 The Department needed to understand the likely future performance of Eurostar UK and put in place a robust financial structure that would enable LCR to meet its obligations. The financial restructuring agreed in 1998 was based on two benchmarks (see **Figure 7**) A "Central Case" assumed construction of the Link to time and budget estimates provided by LCR and that Eurostar UK revenues would grow in line with forecasts prepared for the Department by Booze-Allen & Hamilton. A second set of forecasts was also prepared, below which Eurostar UK financial performance was considered unlikely to fall. This second benchmark is known as the "Downside Case" and was considered as having an 80 per cent chance of being bettered by Eurostar UK. In the event that the Downside Case is not achieved for two consecutive years, the Department has retained a fall-back option of taking Eurostar UK back into public ownership.

2.27 On this basis, the Department put in place an access charge loan facility under which LCR can borrow public funds at a favourable interest rate (LIBOR plus one percentage point) to cover access charge payments by Eurostar UK in the event of a cash shortfall. The amounts involved and the likelihood of their eventual repayment will depend on the performance of Eurostar UK. Such a facility will be required to fill a gap in LCR funds between the time when the finance raised with GGBs to build the Link would be exhausted and the time when Eurostar UK passenger revenues are expected to begin to have a positive effect on LCR cashflow. Under the Government Central Case at the time the deal was restructured in 1998, a cash shortfall of £140 million was forecast between 2010 and 2021. Under other scenarios, however, lending to LCR could range from nil to £360 million. The facility will also provide some flexibility before LCR has to call on one of the guarantees provided by the Government. Extra funding will be made available to generate around £3 million a year of positive cashflow in LCR, after Eurostar UK has paid access charges to Eurotunnel and Railtrack and LCR has met all payments due under the GGBs. This support will be triggered only if LCR has first used all its available financial resources, including any proceeds from property development, for those purposes.

2.28 Under this arrangement, failure to achieve the Downside Case over a period of time could lead to substantial direct lending to LCR, or the reversion of Eurostar UK to public ownership, to avoid calls on the Government guarantees of Eurostar UK access charges and the much larger amounts at risk on the GGBs. This is not a theoretical risk; a revised forecast of Eurostar UK performance, commissioned by the Department in April 2000, indicated that direct lending to LCR was likely to amount to at least £370 million and could, in extreme circumstances, reach £1,200 million. In the face of strong competition from low-cost airlines, which offer an increasingly diverse range of destinations across Europe, Eurostar UK performance has been disappointing. Operational losses in 1999 and 2000 were broadly in line with the losses forecast by the Government's Downside Case (**Figure 15**).

The Government has also guaranteed LCR's potential liabilities on the swaps used to hedge interest rates

2.29 LCR had to consider whether to take action to hedge against future changes in interest rates. Under the terms of the agreements entered into between LCR and Railtrack, LCR has the equivalent of a fixed interest rate receivable in the form of Railtrack's obligation to pay 7 per cent a year on monies provided by LCR to fund the construction of Section 1. The underlying source for this lending is the £1,000 million in proceeds from the issue by LCR of the GGB at a fixed interest rate of 4.75 per cent a year maturing in 2010. However, the actual amount of interest paid by Railtrack to LCR is not fixed and will depend on progress against the construction profile of Section 1 and the exercise of the flexibility allowed to Railtrack in the agreement with LCR governing the timing of the sale of Section 1.

2.30 Railtrack has to purchase Section 1 within one year of completion or by 30 September 2005 or, failing completion of construction, by 31 December 2010. If, as expected, Railtrack purchases Section 1 before the GGB matures in 2010, LCR will have to invest the proceeds at what could be lower rates of interest than had been assumed in the financial model underpinning the

restructured deal. A lower level of interest income could therefore necessitate an increase in the amount of money lent by the Department to LCR to maintain its ability to pay Eurostar UK access charges. On the basis of market expectations for future inflation and associated interest rate changes, SBC Warburg Dillon Read estimated that any additional call on public funds could amount to between £150 million and £300 million.

2.31 The Government and LCR agreed that exposure to a fall in the interest earned on LCR's cash deposits should be hedged through appropriate interest rate swaps. A series of interest rate swaps were therefore put in place by LCR to convert the variable receipt from Railtrack and the fixed interest paid on the 2010 bond to floating rates and maintain the interest rate margin of 2.25 per cent a year LCR would earn as if the timing and quantum of the asset and liability were matched. LCR was responsible for appointing the banks that transacted the swaps and chose SBC Warburg Dillon Read (for two thirds of the business) and Deutsche Bank (for the remaining one third). LCR considered that SBC Warburg Dillon Read had undertaken a significant amount of work in preparation for likely interest rate swaps transactions and, having shared this work with Deutsche Bank, a joint proposal was made by the banks. On the basis of the respective amounts of work undertaken by the banks, LCR determined the split of business between them.

2.32 Benchmarking the price of swaps is difficult in such a large transaction. The Department, through its financial adviser, therefore put in place measures to police the swaps transactions and monitor their pricing in order to ensure that good value would be obtained. Given the

15 **The Department will lend money directly to LCR and will guarantee potential liabilities on LCR's interest rate hedging strategy**

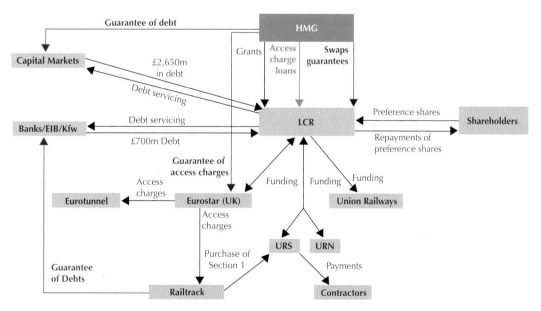

Note: The swaps guarantees will be provided to LCR once the Department has obtained state aid clearance from the European Commission

Source: The Department

complexity of the long-term credit rating of the project, the banks would only enter into interest rate swaps with LCR if it set aside sufficient cash to meet potential payments under the swaps or the Government agreed to guarantee LCR's obligations. The swaps were entered into following the issue of the GGBs on the basis that LCR provided cash collateral in the short term. For the longer term, the Government agreed to provide a guarantee over the remaining life of the swaps, subject to the outcome of a European Commission review of state aid implications. This approach was preferable to the alternative of LCR providing long-term cash collateral of around £150 million, which could have undermined the refinancing plan if, in particular, Eurostar UK revenues did not meet expectations.

But the taxpayer is entitled to future dividends and could sell LCR if Eurostar UK is successful in attracting expected levels of patronage

2.33 In return for Government guarantees and the access charge loan facility, LCR is not allowed to pay dividends on ordinary shares until at least 2021. In the event that LCR is performing well and no longer needs to borrow under the access charge loan facility, the restriction on dividend payments prior to 2021 may be lifted, provided all accumulated borrowing and interest thereon has been repaid. From 2021, the Government is also entitled to receive 35 per cent of LCR's pre-tax cashflow.

This cashflow is first applied to repay any loans outstanding under the access charge loan facility and then is effectively a dividend to Government for providing additional support to LCR. The quantification of these estimated returns is highly subjective, but the Department has estimated that they could be worth some £250 million (**Figure 16**).

2.34 The Department also has a right of veto over a sale of LCR before 2011 and may force the sale or flotation of LCR at any time. On a sale or flotation, the Government would receive 90 per cent of the proceeds, with the remainder (subject to a cap) going to the original shareholders.

16 **The taxpayer is entitled to share in future dividends from LCR**

Note: The swaps guarantees will be provided to LCR once the Department has obtained state aid clearance from the European Commission

Source: The Department

Part 3

The case for public sector support is heavily dependent on wider benefits

This part of the report examines the economic justification for the scale of Government support the Link will receive. It shows that the original project could not have proceeded without public sector grants, and that the Department's case for supporting the project depended on an assessment of whether the economic benefits of the Link would outweigh its costs. The Department estimated passenger benefits and the benefits in terms of economic regeneration that it expected would flow from the Link. In addition, Ministers had regard to wider policy benefits which were not quantified.

Using the Department's own assumptions and methods for quantifying benefits, the estimated net benefits of the Link are worth some £1,000 million. But there is scope for debate about this calculation. On a conventional basis the outcome would have been much lower. Moreover, Eurostar UK performance has so far been well below that envisaged in the Government Central Case. This implies that the benefits would be lower and the costs higher than in the Department's estimate. What this means is that the economic justification for public grants to support the project is heavily dependent on the wider policy benefits envisaged by the Government.

Public sector support for the Link was inevitable

3.1 The Government has been involved throughout the development of the Link. It was obliged to promote and progress the Channel Tunnel Rail Link Act through Parliament under the Channel Tunnel Rail Link Development Agreement, which forms part of the contract with LCR. The Act received Royal Assent in December 1996.

The public sector is necessarily involved through regulation and through integration with the existing rail network

3.2 The Secretary of State for the Environment, Transport and the Regions is responsible, through the Health and Safety Executive, for ensuring that the Link will meet safety standards, as required for the rest of the rail network. The Link is being constructed to meet international high-speed railway safety standards and the line is to be equipped with automatic train protection signalling. Discussions are ongoing with HM Railway Inspectorate to ensure that the detailed design and construction of the Link meets safety requirements. Railtrack and, if Railtrack does not exercise its option, the infrastructure owner of Section 2 will have to produce a Railway Safety Case, which must be accepted by the Railway Inspectorate, before each section of the new line can open for commercial services.

3.3 The Link will be used by domestic services as well as Eurostar UK services and the Secretary of State has a contractual right under the Development Agreement to approve domestic services. Although domestic services will not be subject to regulation for the parts of a journey that are on the Link, the Rail Regulator will be responsible for approving those parts of the services that run on the national network. Trains used for domestic services and Eurostar trains may also need to use parts of the national network in an emergency or during engineering works and must therefore be technically compatible with those parts of the network.

The project also involves international obligations and working with the state railways of Belgium and France

3.4 In addition to the domestic obligations on the Government, there are international obligations on the UK under the Channel Tunnel Usage Contract 1987, which governs the use of the Channel Tunnel itself. These oblige the UK and French governments to provide sufficient passenger and freight rail infrastructure to meet forecast demand for use of the Tunnel. At the time the Usage Contract was agreed, the UK's obligations stated that investment in such infrastructure had to meet British Rail's investment appraisal criteria.

3.5 Eurostar services are jointly operated by Eurostar UK and the French and Belgian State railways. As a private sector train operator, Eurostar UK has greater commercial incentives to compete effectively and maximise revenues and profits than do the two state-owned companies. Joint operation has, in the past, reduced Eurostar UK's flexibility to respond to changes in the market. However, the three companies are now operating together under a new joint management structure, Eurostar Group, which is intended to improve co-ordination of objectives and marketing strategies.

But there were no obligations to build a fast Link

3.6 Although the Channel Tunnel Usage Contract obliges the Government to provide sufficient infrastructure to meet forecast demand for use of the Tunnel, there is no obligation to build a high-speed link. The obligations require journey times between London and Paris to be between 2 hours 55 minutes and 3 hours 5 minutes. Current Eurostar UK performance meets these obligations with the existing rail network. Furthermore, track and signalling improvements undertaken since the opening of the Channel Tunnel have allowed direct services to be quicker than the requirements. According to passenger forecasts carried out for the Government's value for money assessment, the existing network and the capacity of the Waterloo International terminal, with minor upgrades, should be sufficient to meet international demand until around 2025. However, there would be a need for extra capacity on the network if the expected increase in demand for domestic services was to be met.

Given the high capital costs and uncertainty over future revenues, a Government subsidy would be needed

3.7 At an estimated construction cost in excess of £4,000 million, the Link is one of the largest infrastructure projects in Europe. The main source of income to recover this enormous investment is Eurostar UK revenues. These depend on the number of passengers using the Eurostar UK services and the fares they will be willing to pay. With such large public transport infrastructure projects, it is unlikely that the cost of construction can be recovered over a reasonable length of time from fares paid by passengers. In the case of the Link, factors such as competition with airlines limit the fares that Eurostar UK can charge and still attract passengers. Appendix 6 explains why costs are unlikely to be recovered solely through passenger revenues.

3.8 This means the Link was unlikely to be built without some form of financial support from the public sector. Under the original competition for the Link, LCR and other bidders estimated the expected costs of constructing and operating the Link and the revenues from Eurostar UK over the contract period. The difference between these figures determined the "Funding Gap", which represented the level of public sector financial support required.

The Department's stated objectives allowed it to subsidise the Link if it was economically justified

3.9 The Department decided to back the construction of the Link if it could be demonstrated that the estimated benefits would outweigh the estimated level of public sector financial support. The Department's stated objectives were:

a) to more than double the capacity of four trains per hour (three in the evening peak) available for international passenger railway services between London and the Channel Tunnel;

b) to reduce the journey time of those services between London and the Channel Tunnel by about half an hour to about 40 minutes;

c) to provide greater capacity and reduced journey times for domestic passengers; and

d) to contribute to the regeneration of the Thames Gateway.

3.10 The main benefits to justify the support arise from these objectives. Passengers will benefit from the increase in capacity and from the savings in journey times due to the increased speed of Eurostar and domestic services. Further, the Government estimates that benefits will arise from the regeneration of the Thames Gateway, through which the second stage of the Link will run. These objectives have not changed since the original deal was signed in 1996.

The amount of direct subsidy required will be at least £1,800 million

3.11 The Government agreed to provide direct grants to fund construction of the Link as both an international and domestic railway. **Figure 17** outlines the types of grant involved.

17 **The types of public grants for the Link**

Type of grant	Amount (£ millions)
Direct grants: construction	1,619
Direct grants: domestic capacity	395
TOTAL GRANTS	**2,014**
Less: Land rentals (note)	(266)
NET TOTAL	1,748

Note: Land rental payments will be made to the Government, beginning in 2030.

Source: The Department

3.12 In addition to the direct grants, the Government has provided guarantees to bond investors and has agreed to lend additional funds to LCR to enable Eurostar UK to meet its access charge commitments in the event that revenues do not meet expectations. Additional subsidy will also be paid, initially by the Department and later by the Strategic Rail Authority to support domestic services using the Link. The total amount of public sector support for the project therefore exceeds the present value of the direct grants to be paid by the Department.

The Department estimated that the economic and wider benefits would outweigh the subsidy, so support for the Link was economically justified

3.13 The Department undertook value for money assessments to determine whether the Link would deliver sufficient benefits to justify the level of public sector support involved. The main benefits included in the assessments accrue to international and domestic passengers and therefore depend on the number of passengers using the train services. LCR based its bid on the number of passengers expected to travel on Eurostar UK over the assessment period. During the original competition in 1996, the Department did not undertake an independent assessment of LCR's or other bidders' passenger forecasts. At the time, the Department considered that previous passenger forecasts prepared

in conjunction with British Rail were consistent with LCR's projections and could be relied on. However, all the forecasts used were over-optimistic and the failure to achieve them contributed towards the near collapse of the original deal.

3.14 LCR revised its forecasts downward for the restructured deal in 1998. However, the Department employed transport consultants Booze-Allen & Hamilton to provide an independent review of the revised forecasts and to produce their own forecasts of Eurostar UK patronage and revenues, upon which the Department could base its value for money assessment.

3.15 Booze-Allen &Hamilton produced forecasts for two main scenarios. A Government Central Case, which was somewhat lower than LCR's Management Case, formed the basis of the value for money assessment and the main calculation of the level of public sector support. A Government Downside Case represented a more pessimistic scenario, which was used to test whether public support for the Link was still justified if fewer passengers than expected use Eurostar UK services.

3.16 Booze-Allen & Hamilton's forecasts were based on annual patronage levels. To consider what these forecasts meant in practical terms, we calculated the daily passenger figures implied by the Government Central Case forecasts along with the number of full trains required, assuming each train was either full or operating at Eurostar UK's target of 65 per cent of capacity. The Department told us that the average number of Eurostar trains a day in 1999 was 52, carrying an average of 350 passengers (45 per cent of capacity) giving a total patronage in 1999 of 6.6 million. This compared with a forecast for 1999 of 7.4 million passengers. The results for the years 2010, 2020 and 2030 are shown in **Figure 18**.

18 **Breakdown of annual patronage assumptions into daily figures**

Breakdown	Year		
	2010	2020	2030
Forecast annual passenger levels	13.8 million	19.5 million	25.8 million
Passengers per day (363 day year)	38,000	53,800	71,100
Number of capacity filled train journeys per day required to meet forecast demand, 363 days of the year, assuming an average of 778 passengers a train	49	69	91
Number of 65 per cent full train journeys per day required to meet forecast demand, 363 days of the year, assuming an average of 506 passengers per train	75	106	141
Number of 45 per cent full train journeys per day required to meet forecast demand, 363 days of the year, assuming an average of 350 passengers a train	109	153	203

Note: Based on a 14 hour day

Source: National Audit Office, Booze-Allen & Hamilton

3.17 To meet the demand forecasts on which the restructured deal was based, an average of 69 capacity filled train journeys would need to run between London and Paris or Brussels every day for 363 days in 2020, equivalent to one full train every 12 minutes (106 train journeys a day at 65 per cent of capacity, or one train every 8 minutes). If Eurostar UK trains continue to run at 45 per cent of capacity, as in 1999, this would require 153 train journeys a day in 2020. This would be nearly three times the average daily number of train journeys in 1999 and would equate to one train every 5½ minutes.

3.18 The final Government Central Case estimate of May 1998 showed that the total public sector contribution to the project was £2,300 million, including the access charge loan facility and subsidies by the Office of Passenger Rail Franchising[9], and the total benefits were "around £3,000 million". The Department also estimated that the deal meant the Department would avoid £300 million of net costs which it would incur if Eurostar UK reverted to public sector operation. The Department estimated the final net present value to be around £1,000 million, with a benefit cost ratio of 1.5:1. The full Government Central Case assessment is shown in **Figure 19**.

3.19 The Government Downside Case was also shown to be justified, but the Department recognised that this was very marginal with a benefit cost ratio of only 1.1:1. In addition to the main value for money assessments, the Department undertook Cost Benefit analyses of several alternative options to the Link, such as delaying the project for ten years, only building Section 1, and undertaking relatively minor capacity improvements to the existing network. These calculations were not prepared in as much detail as the main value for money assessment as the Department did not have as much cost information. The assessments indicated, however, that delaying the project by ten years and improving the capacity of the existing network provided less absolute benefits but more favourable benefit to cost ratios than the existing project, because of reduced or delayed costs.

3.20 The three main benefits included by the Department were international and domestic non-financial passenger benefits (international and domestic passenger benefits) and regeneration benefits. The Department believes that international and domestic passenger benefits arise through reduced journey times and increased rail capacity and that regeneration benefits arise from the impact of the Link in attracting jobs to the areas through which it will run , particularly in the Thames Gateway and near areas surrounding the three international stations at St. Pancras, Stratford and Ebbsfleet.

3.21 The government has a number of more conventional funding mechanisms, which are specifically designed to create jobs and regenerate priority areas, such as through English Partnerships and the Single

19 | **The final Government Central Case value for money assessment of May 1998**

The figure shows that the government estimated that the Link is economically justified under the Government Central Case

Type of benefit/cost	Government Central Case (£ million, present value[1])
Benefits	
International non-financial benefits	1800
Domestic non-financial benefits	1000
Road decongestion	30
Environmental freight benefits	90
Regeneration benefits	500
Reduced Thameslink 2000	0
Total benefits	**"around £3000"**
Costs	
LUL and A2/M2 costs[2]	0
Government direct grants (less land rentals)	(1800)
Access charge loan facility	(100)
Office of Passenger Rail Franchising subsidy	(400)
Net Eurostar UK revenue foregone	(440)
Repayments of Eurostar UK debt	400
Additional costs of Thameslink 2000	240
Project wind up costs	110
Total net Government contribution	**(1,990)**
Net present value	**1,010**
Benefit cost ratio	**1.5:1**

Notes: 1 The Department's value for money assessment rounded the figures for benefits and costs. In particular, the estimated total benefits figure was rounded down by some £400 million in recognition of the inevitable uncertainties surrounding such estimates.

2 Under the Channel Tunnel Rail Link Act 1996, powers were secured to upgrade part of the A2/M2 which runs parallel to the route of the Link.

Source: The Department

Regeneration Budget. For the value for money assessment, the Department estimated the amount the Government would need to spend using these more conventional means to create the same number of jobs as the Department estimated the Link would create. This "willingness to pay" figure formed the estimate of the Link's regeneration benefits. More detailed descriptions of these benefits are given in Appendix 7.

3.22 Other benefits were also estimated, such as environmental benefits arising from freight transfer from road to rail and road decongestion benefits as people opted to travel on Eurostar UK rather than flying or driving. We have not been able to confirm the reasonableness of these estimates as the Department was unable to locate detailed evidence supporting these calculations. The Department also calculated the net costs of Eurostar UK reversion saved by accepting the deal, including engineering work for the

9   *Now the Strategic Rail Authority*

Thameslink 2000 project and London Underground work, the repayment of Eurostar UK debt, and the costs avoided by delaying the project. An estimate of the potential Eurostar UK revenues the Government was foregoing by leaving the business in the private sector was also included as a cost of the deal. However, as with any appraisal many estimates are uncertain. For example, fewer benefits will accrue and the Government will forego less net revenues if fewer passengers use Eurostar UK than estimated, impacting adversely on the value for money case. Passenger figures to date have been lower than forecast and we discuss the impact on the value for money of the Link if this continues to be the case in paragraphs 3.36 to 3.40 below.

The government recognised wider but unquantified policy benefits from the Link

3.23 In addition to the quantified estimates of economic benefits, the Department expects that the Link will lead to wider benefits, which have not been quantified. The Government sees the project as one of national prestige as it provides a high speed rail service to Europe. France and Belgium already have such links to the Channel Tunnel, and the Link is one of a number of high priority projects for the development of high speed rail routes across the EU known as the Trans-European Transport Network. This has given the Link priority status in the Government's overall transport policy and led to support from the European Investment Bank. Although such a consideration was not formally included in the Department's stated objectives, it was an important consideration in Ministerial announcements on the project.

The Department's economic assessment of the project is debatable

The Department made changes to the value for money assessment as the deal progressed

3.24 The Department made changes to the value for money assessments as more information became available. The first major value for money assessment was made in March 1998. This was amended in April 1998 to include estimates of the costs of allowing Eurostar UK to revert to public ownership, and the fare revenues the Government was foregoing by accepting the LCR deal and not operating the service in the public sector.

3.25 The final assessment by the Department in May 1998 showed that the public sector support for the Link was justified and formed the basis of the Deputy Prime Minister's announcement to Parliament the following month of the key elements of the restructured deal with LCR. The final assessment resulted from more information becoming available. For example, modelling results for benefits and subsidy requirements for

domestic services, which were received from the Office of Passenger Rail Franchising[7]. The costs of Eurostar UK reversion, including estimates of net revenues and debt repayments were also re-estimated as more information on operating costs became available. These showed that Eurostar UK operating costs were higher than previously estimated and the net revenues foregone by restructuring the deal were much lower than in the April 1998 estimate, improving the value for money case.

3.26 Other changes in the May 1998 assessment reflected changes in methodology. These included:

- the removal of international benefits to non-UK residents, in line with Treasury guidance, which reduced total benefits by some £1,800 million; and

- the introduction of monetary estimates of regeneration benefits, which increased benefits by some £500 million.

The final methodology was unconventional for a public transport project at that time

3.27 There is no clear and agreed methodology for calculating the monetary impacts of the wider benefits of public transport projects, such as the regeneration of local economies, so they are not usually included in monetary terms in the value for money assessments of such projects. The impacts may be positive or negative, and should be considered on a case by case basis. The Link is the first new international railway project to be assessed by the Department, and the international aspects of the project raised issues not normally considered in the appraisal of domestic transport projects. It is understandable, therefore, that the Department should have considered impacts which have not been assessed in other public transport project appraisals. On this basis, the Department judged that the regeneration benefits expected from this project were likely to be positive and that monetary estimates of these impacts should be included in the final value for money assessment of May 1998.

3.28 The first value for money assessment of the restructured deal in March 1998 reflected more closely the Department's traditional approach to appraisal of domestic transport projects in that monetary estimates of regeneration benefits were not included. This was because the Department believed that to a large extent they represent the double counting of benefits to passengers which were already scored as a component of international and domestic benefits. The assessment also referred to a recent report by the Government's Standing Advisory Committee on Trunk Road Appraisal (SACTRA). This stated that "there are strong theoretical expectations that all or a part of a transport cost reduction will lead to economic impacts outside the transport sector, but the empirical evidence of the scale and significance of such impacts is weak and disputed".

The report also stated that regeneration impacts should be considered on a case by case basis but it did not recommend that monetary values should be included.

3.29 The Department decided, however, that its methodology for estimating a monetary value for regeneration benefits in this case was sufficiently robust to allow their inclusion in the value for money assessment. The Department estimated that the government would be willing to pay £1,000 million through conventional regeneration funding routes to create the number of jobs the Link was expected to create (see Appendix 7 for a more detailed description). The Department then halved this figure to take account of double counting of benefits already reflected in the international passenger benefits to UK residents. This resulted in estimated regeneration benefits from non-UK residents of about £500 million. Including this figure helped to keep the value for money assessment positive by partially compensating for the removal of the estimated £1,800 million of international passenger benefits to Non-UK residents. If the Department had not included an estimate of regeneration benefits quantified in money terms in the final assessment, some other form of assessment of the regeneration benefits would have been used to inform Ministers of the estimated impact of the project on regeneration. For example, in previous assessments, the number of jobs expected to be created and increases in work floor space had been used.

3.30 The quantification and use of monetary values to assess the regeneration benefits of the Link resulted from the need to provide specific and detailed advice on a major transport project, which the Department judged to have major regeneration impacts. However, current economic appraisal guidance issued by the Department still states that regeneration benefits should be taken into account, but that methodologies are too uncertain to produce a monetary value. More recent and current Departmental guidance requires the production of an Appraisal Summary Table, which notes whether the project is in a designated regeneration area and whether any project dependent development sites exist. The decision-maker then uses judgement to assess this information against other impacts presented in the table. Following on from recommendations made by SACTRA, the Department is undertaking research on guidance on more generalised quantification of regeneration benefits for use in transport appraisals.

There was no explicit guidance on the inclusion of passenger benefits

3.31 At the time of this deal, the Department did not have explicit guidance for the appraisal of new heavy rail schemes to complement the guidance it had issued for light rail schemes (such as trams). As a result, some of

the assumptions made by the Department are questionable. Guidance for new heavy rail schemes such as the Link did not exist because the vast majority of public support for heavy rail was for maintenance and improvement of existing services through the Public Service Obligation prior to the privatisation of British Rail and, following privatisation, through franchise payments. However, the assessments undertaken by British Rail and the Department of the few new heavy rail projects had, in practice, included benefits to passengers, such as time savings and improvements in capacity. These projects were not expected to be able to capture all the passenger benefits through fares.

3.32 Following consultations[10], the Franchising Director issued guidance on appraising passenger rail services in May 1999[11]. This describes the appraisal criteria applied to the assessment of changes to passenger rail services supported by the Franchising Director. The guidance states that fares alone should be the most commonly used indicator of user (passenger) benefits. However, where fares are regulated or capacity constrained, there are likely to be some benefits that are not wholly captured in revenue. These can then be included as part of the scheme's justification. In the Department's view the Franchising Director's guidance was not applicable to the Link, other than for considering the support to be given to domestic services which would use the track, and did not constrain the decision criteria applied by Ministers. The Department issued revised guidance on "Multi-Modal Appraisal" in March 2000, which states that estimates of passenger benefits can be included in appraisals of all road and rail projects. This guidance does not replace the Franchising Director's guidance as it applies largely to transport schemes outside the Director's remit.

3.33 The Department included an estimate of the benefits to international passengers resident in the UK in the value for money assessment. These consist of capacity benefits and time saving benefits (explained in Appendix 7), above those that can be captured through fares. This implies that the operator cannot set fares at levels which will capture user benefits in full as enough passengers are not willing to pay for the time saving benefits they are expected to derive from using the Link.

3.34 If Eurostar UK fares were increased to reflect the time savings, it is likely that many passengers would use alternative means of travelling or choose not to travel at all. Eurostar UK competes with airlines operating between London, Paris and Brussels and other destinations, and to a lesser extent, with ferries travelling the cross-Channel route. These other transport modes operate without government subsidy, and indeed, airline passengers must pay a departure tax. The Department decided that it was worth supporting the project in order to provide the international and domestic passenger

10   *Appraisal of Support for Passenger Rail Services - A Consultation Paper (November 1996)*
11   *Planning Criteria: A Guide to the Appraisal of Support for Passenger Rail Services, May 1999 (Interim Guidance was issued in November 1997)*

benefits, as only by doing this could the wider benefits be provided to those not using the service. Without public sector support, either the Link would not be built or the fare levels would be so high that fewer passengers would use the service. The Department believes that this would mean that the estimated regeneration, and other benefits to non-users would not arise.

Some of the assumptions in the value for money assessment are questionable

3.35 There are a number of aspects of the value for money assessment which are questionable (Appendix 8 describes our concerns at (a) to (c) below in more detail):

a) the Department used out of date economic growth assumptions to estimate time saving benefits. The rate used was 2.4 per cent[12] a year, which is higher than the rates recommended in the Department's own guidance, 2.17 per cent until 2016 and 2.21 per cent thereafter[13]. This means that the time saving benefits were overestimated. In the value for money assessment of March 1998, the Department noted that the impact on the appraisal of small changes in value of time growth is quite marked;

b) the assessment made incorrect assumptions of the amount of time savings by assuming that all Eurostar services would benefit from average time savings of around 30 minutes following the opening of the Link. However, following the opening of the Link, about one third of services are expected to continue to use Waterloo terminal so will only benefit from time savings from Section 1 of around 20 minutes, as these journeys will use the existing track between the end of Section 1 and Waterloo. Adjusting these figures to more accurately represent the split between Waterloo and St. Pancras reduces the overall estimate of time saving benefits;

c) in the May 1998 assessment, the Department removed costs of £130 million for the King's Cross Northern ticket hall London Underground works and road works on the A2 and M2, which depend on the Link and had been included in earlier value for money assessments. These costs should have been retained in the final assessment. Indeed, following discussions with the Department these cost estimates have been increased to £170 million;

d) the calculations are not consistent with LCR's assumptions. If Eurostar UK attracts the number of passengers forecast in later years , there will not be sufficient rolling stock to carry them. For example, forecasts show that 25.8 million passengers are expected in 2030, requiring around 59 trains. The forecast Eurostar UK fleet is only 46 trains. The Department accepts there is an inconsistency in that some provision for the purchase of additional rolling stock should have been made.

The value for money justification for public sector support is marginal if amended assumptions are used

3.36 We have re-estimated the May 1998 value for money assessment using patronage and fare figures from the Government Central Case, but with the following amended assumptions:

■ we used the Department's recommended economic growth assumptions to calculate growth in time saving benefits;

■ time saving estimates were adjusted to assume one third of Eurostar services continue to use Waterloo, so only benefiting from Section 1 time savings of 20 minutes;

■ the Department was unable to provide the detailed calculations used to estimate road decongestion and environmental freight benefits (non-user transport benefits). We could not verify them and have therefore calculated the total net present value with and without these benefits;

■ costs of £170 million have been included for London Underground and A2 works following discussions with the Department;

■ we removed the regeneration benefits as current guidance states that these should be considered but not quantified in money terms. In view of its decision to remove time saving benefits for non-UK residents from the calculations, the Department believes that the methodology adopted was robust and appropriate. However, the Department also accepts that the use of monetary values cannot be supported by any published departmental appraisal guidance.

---

12   This rate was recommended by Highways Economics Note No 2 issued in September 1996
13   These rates were included in guidance issued in November 1997

3.37 **Figure 20** shows that these adjustments reduce the net present value of the project from the Government's figure of around £1,000 million to some £220 million, with a benefit-cost ratio of 1.1:1. We calculate that if Eurostar UK performs just nine per cent below the Government Central Case, the net present value of the Link falls to zero. If the figures for non-user transport benefits are excluded, the net present value is only £120 million, with a benefit to cost ratio of just over 1:1. If Eurostar UK performs at just four per cent below forecast passenger numbers, the net present value falls to zero. Patronage on Eurostar UK in 1999 was 6.6 million, some 10 per cent lower than the Government Central Case forecast of 7.4 million.

3.38 If the Department's estimate of regeneration benefits is included, the net present value rises to some £720 million, with a benefit-cost ratio of 1.3:1, some £300 million lower than the Department's estimate.

The value for money justification for public sector support collapses if Eurostar UK does not achieve expected patronage levels

3.39 The Government Downside Case in the March 1998 value for money assessment was marginally positive, with international benefits estimated at around 70 per cent of the Government Central Case. Though no downside case assessment was presented in May 1998, we have estimated a downside case by reducing the international benefits to 70 per cent of those in the

20   **National Audit Office reworking of May 1998 Government Central Case**

The figure shows that the economic justification for the Link is marginal, at some £220 million, with a benefit-cost ratio of just 1.1:1, if corrected assumptions are used and regeneration benefits are excluded in line with current guidance. This compares with the government's assessment of £1,000 million and a benefit-cost ratio of 1.5:1. If the figures for road decongestion and environmental freight benefits are removed, the net present value falls to £100 million, a benefit to cost ratio of just over 1:1.

	Government Central Case (£ millions rounded, present value)	NAO assessment (£ millions rounded, present value), excluding regeneration benefits
Benefits		
International non-financial benefits	1800	1450
Domestic non-financial benefits[1]	1000	800
Road decongestion[2]	30	30
Environmental freight benefits[2]	90	90
Regeneration benefits	500	0
Reduced Thameslink 2000 benefits	0	(100)
Total benefits	**"around £3000"**	**2270**
Costs		
London Underground Ltd and A2/M2	0	(170)
Government direct grants (less land rentals)	(1800)	(1800)
Access charge loan facility	(100)	(140)
Office of Passenger Rail Franchising subsidy	(400)	(250)
Net Eurostar UK revenue foregone	(440)	(440)
Repayments of Eurostar UK debt	400	400
Additional costs of Thameslink 2000	240	240
Project wind up costs	110	110
Total net Government contribution	**(1,990)**	**(2,050)**
NPV	**1,010**	**220**
Benefit cost ratio	**1.5:1**	**1.1:1**

Notes: 1. The Department told us that recent estimates of this figure suggest it may be an overestimate, but the results are not yet final. The figure used is the one available to the Department in May 1998.

        2. The Department could not provide the detailed calculations of non-user transport benefits, so we are unable to confirm these figures.

If the Department's estimate of regeneration benefits is included, the net present value increases to £720 million, some £300 million lower than the Department's estimate. These figures are explained in detail in Appendices 7 and 8.

Source: The Department, National Audit Office

Central Case and replacing the Government Central Case access charge loan estimate of £140 million with the £360 million estimated for the Downside case. The revised net present value is -£450 million, excluding regeneration benefits. If the non-user transport benefits are excluded, this falls further to -£570 million.

3.40 We also estimated the Government Downside Case, including regeneration benefits of £350 million, 70 per cent of the £500 million included in the Government Central Case[14]. This increases the net present value to -£100 million (or -£220 million if road decongestion and environmental freight benefits are excluded). We consider that the Link would not be economically justified in the Government Downside Case, even if the Department's estimate of regeneration benefits is included. In April 2000, Booze-Allen & Hamilton revised their forecasts, based on the actual performance of Eurostar UK. This work showed that patronage is currently below the forecasts in the March 1998 Government Downside Case. Booze-Allen & Hamilton also stated that the Government Downside Case should now be seen as an achievable target for an Upside Case. If Eurostar UK continues to perform at or below the Government Downside Case estimates, then the economic justification for the Link collapses. This means that the justification for the Link is heavily dependent on the wider and unquantified policy benefits that the project is thought to bring.

14   In the absence of figures from the Department, this implies there is a direct link between patronage and the level of regeneration benefits. The Department considers that some regeneration benefits will occur as a result of the Link's construction, irrespective of the number of passengers, but were unable to provide estimates.

Appendix 1 Chronology of key events

1994

March   The Department issues pre-qualification documents for the Link project. Nine consortia respond to the invitation.

June   Four consortia pre-qualify and are invited to submit full proposals.

1995

June   LCR and Eurorail CTRL Limited are short-listed.

December LCR and Eurorail CTRL Limited submit their final bids.

1996

February The Department and LCR sign the contract for the project.

May   The contract becomes fully effective and the Department transfers to LCR the Government-owned companies Union Railways Limited and European Passenger Services Limited (later renamed Eurostar (UK) Limited).

November Fire in the Channel Tunnel seriously damages the lining of one of the two running tunnels.

December Royal assent of the Channel Tunnel Rail Link Bill.

1997

February Department receives a notice from LCR stating that second stage financing would be delayed from October 1997 to April 1998 but that LCR would exhaust its funds from the first stage financing in January 1998. LCR proposes bridging this funding gap by selling Eurostar train sets and leasing them back from the new owner.

June   LCR provides the Department with a draft report documenting the findings of L.E.K. Consulting on future Eurostar UK patronage.

July   Ministers meet LCR to discuss bridging the funding gap in its finances.

August Department sends a letter to LCR setting out the terms upon which the Department would agree to the sale and lease back of the Eurostar train sets.

September LCR receives the full report from L.E.K. Consulting and realises that Eurostar UK may lose £750 million more in the medium-term than forecast. The scale of the expected loss puts the second stage financing beyond LCR's reach. LCR enters into extensive discussions with the Department.

        LCR also enters into discussions with Railtrack to ascertain its appetite for becoming involved in the project.

1998

January LCR breaks off negotiations with Railtrack and approaches the Department with a request for an additional £1,200 million[15] of direct grants. The Department rejects LCR's request but, in accordance with the contract, grants it a cure period of 30 days to prepare a more acceptable rescue package.

February LCR presents the outline of a proposal that the Department finds acceptable enough to grant an extension to the cure period.
        The Department allows LCR to sell and leaseback its Eurostar trainsets.

June   The Deputy Prime Minister announces that the Department, LCR and Railtrack have signed a Statement of Principles for restructuring the project.

October Construction starts of Section 1 of the Link.

1999

February Following state aid clearance with the European Commission, Government-guaranteed bonds are issued by LCR.
        Restructured deal implemented.

15   1995 prices

Appendix 2

Scope and methodology of the National Audit Office's examination

Scope of this study

1. We examined whether the Department achieved its objectives in negotiations with LCR and other parties on the structure of the project.

Main aspects of the National Audit Office's methodology

2. Our examination covered:

   - The conduct of the negotiations: how the Department went about the task.

     The purpose of this part of the examination was to assess whether the Department's approach was well planned and implemented.

   - Outcome: how far the outcome should meet the objectives.

     This part of the examination focused on the extent to which the restructured deal should meet the Department's objectives and whether it provides value for money.

3. In undertaking this examination we followed the approach laid out in a published report on our methodology for examining private finance deals.[16] In particular, we:

   - Designed the examination using experience acquired on our earlier studies of Private Finance Initiative deals;

   - Collected information about the negotiation process and the deal;

   - Used an external expert to advise on specific issues; and

   - Evaluated the information and advice received.

Collection of information

4. We collected information from the following sources:

   - A review of the Department's papers recording the negotiations and of the legal agreements underpinning the deal;

   - Interviews with Departmental officials and advisers, on how they handled the negotiation of the deal;

   - Discussions with the key private sector participants in the restructured deal (LCR, Railtrack and ICRR).

Use of external expertise

5. We engaged RBC Dominion Securities (a part of the Royal Bank of Canada Group) to examine the arrangements put in place to finance the restructured deal and advise on how well they met the Department's objectives while offering value for money.

---

16   *Examining the value for money of deals under the Private Finance Initiative (HC 739/1998-99)*

Appendix 3

Additional information on the Link

1. In 1984, an Anglo-French consortium, Eurotunnel, received the concession to build and operate the Channel Tunnel between the United Kingdom and France. Financed by the private sector, it opened ten years later. Besides carrying a shuttle service between terminals at each end for road vehicles and their passengers, the Tunnel also provides for through passenger and freight rail services. From November 1994, passenger services were operated jointly by European Passenger Services Ltd (EPSL), SNCF and SNCB (the state-owned railways of France and Belgium respectively) with routes from London (Waterloo) to Paris and Brussels. Freight services through the Channel Tunnel are operated by Railfreight Distribution[17], which is owned by English, Welsh & Scottish Railways.

2. British Rail (and subsequently Railtrack) as well as the train operators invested a total of £1,500 million in infrastructure works and rolling stock to accommodate these additional passenger and freight services. However, the Department of Transport's "Kent Impact Study" in 1987 recognised the need for extra rail capacity in the South East and in 1988, following a British Rail study, tenders were invited for the design and construction of a new rail link from the Channel Tunnel to London.

3. Eurorail, a consortium comprising Trafalgar House and BICC, was awarded the concession as part of a joint venture with British Rail. The route it promoted approached London from the South East, broadly following the M20/A20 corridor as far as Hither Green. From there, a tunnelling scheme was to provide access to both Waterloo and a terminus proposed in the King's Cross area. By the middle of 1991, however, the Government considered that the proposed route would not realise the full potential of the international connection for London, nor provide any significant regeneration benefits. Furthermore, the route would have had a considerable environmental impact on south-east London. In October 1991, the Government announced that an approach to London from the east was preferred. The northern half of the British Rail/Eurorail route was abandoned in favour of a Thames crossing of some kind in the Dartford area and then an approach roughly along the A13 corridor before entering tunnelling to terminate, again, around King's Cross.

Private finance studies, 1991-93

4. The joint venture route required £1,900 million of public sector money to be either committed or placed at risk during the early stages of construction. The Government felt that some of the risks could be better managed by the private sector and therefore decided that the project should proceed as part of the Private Finance Initiative (PFI).

5. In December 1991, the then Department of Transport formed a team to consider ways of involving the private sector and to propose a structure which would make the most of what a private sector promoter could offer. The investment bank, Samuel Montagu and civil engineers W.S. Atkins were appointed as consultants, while the Private Finance Panel of the Bank of England participated in the development of the policy. Between then and the end of 1993, this team reviewed the key features of other private finance projects and identified the factors which contributed to their success. The work also included a consultation exercise and a number of other studies in order to understand what the private sector would be looking for in a project like the Link and to determine how best to incentivise an eventual promoter to deliver the results the Government wanted.

6. During this time, Union Railways Limited (URL), which was then a British Rail agency company, was responsible for refining the route corridor announced by the Secretary of State in October 1991 into an alignment sufficiently detailed to be placed before Ministers and then Parliament. This involved examining route alternatives totalling more than ten times the actual route length. A few options were then subjected to further refinement with a report to Government in March 1993 being followed by public consultation and a further report in October of that year. In January 1994 the Government then took a number of decisions in principle on the route based on the results of this work. URL's work throughout was supported with a grant from the European Commission under the Trans-European Networks (TENs) programme. Once the route was determined in sufficient detail in early 1994, safeguarding was carried out to protect it from conflicting planning proposals and the drafting of a Hybrid Bill was put in hand.

17   *Now called EWS International*

The competition to choose a promoter for the Link

7. Having decided that the design, build, finance, operation and maintenance of the link would be the responsibility of a private sector company, the then Government invited bids from the private sector. The competition aimed to allow bidders to manage the risks of the project and to create flexibility for potential private sector promoters. The Government was best placed to manage legislative risk, given the need for a Hybrid Bill to be passed to provide the necessary powers to construct and operate a transport infrastructure of this magnitude. It also specified minimum requirements (e.g. international train speeds of at least 225km/h on high speed sections) and made strategic decisions on issues such as the choice of route, but overall a framework was provided that allowed scope for innovation by the private sector.

8. As part of the proposed contract, the Government decided that EPSL would be transferred to the private sector promoter. As well as being a source of revenue for the promoter, this allowed a vertically integrated approach to be taken with respect to the provision of railway infrastructure and the operation of trains. While this contrasted with the domestic rail privatisation approach, the Department considered that the issues surrounding international services were quite distinct.

9. The studies undertaken between 1991 and 1993 had shown that a revenue stream from an existing service could make a valuable contribution to new infrastructure costs by putting money into the enterprise well before construction was complete, and at a time when raising debt and equity finance would still be expensive because of the high risks involved. It was felt that the two activities were so entirely inter-dependent on each other, that the same company should have control of both operations.

10. Also to be transferred to the private sector promoter was URL, which had designed and promoted the link route. The reasoning behind the transfer was not financial, but because of the intellectual property held by URL. By transferring URL, the promoter would then be able to take the design and promotion forward. EPSL, URL and certain other assets such as development land were therefore transferred from British Rail to direct Government ownership in preparation for the award of the Link contract. The Government laid down specific criteria in respect of how the promoter would be selected:

   ■ the amount of Government grant required;

   ■ the willingness of the private sector to take on risk.

11. In February 1994, a notice appeared in the Official Journal of the European Community announcing the launch of the competition. Expressions of interest were invited and nine consortia responded. Meanwhile, the Hybrid Bill to authorise the Link was introduced to Parliament in November 1994. The House of Commons convened a Select Committee, which had the power to require changes to the project, following its consideration of petitioners' cases during 1995. A similar process was undertaken in the House of Lords.

Involvement of the private sector

12. It had always been widely recognised that the Link would never be viable as a wholly privately financed project. The revenue stream from Eurostar UK services would not be sufficient by itself to make the project viable for a private sector company and therefore some element of public support was necessary. Furthermore, there were of many wider benefits to be gained, including the regeneration of the Thames Gateway and the improvement in London's competitiveness as a business centre through better transport infrastructure. Accordingly, the Government of the day pledged a substantial contribution to the construction cost of the project, but made clear that it wanted to know how much it would be required to commit and when. The Government expected most of the construction to be finished before it would begin to pay its share because this would provide the assurance that substantial amounts of private sector finance were being invested and placed at risk. As a further assurance, the payments of public sector grant instalments were to be conditional upon the achievement of specified milestones in the project programme.

13. The European Union (EU) also made clear its commitment to the project. Since 1992 URL's work has been supported by the Trans-European Networks programme, to support development work on projects which connect the growing network of high-speed railways between major European centres. The European Investment Bank (EIB) was another important player with the Link being the kind of project which it is designed to support. The EIB provides loans for capital investment, thereby supporting the EU's aim for balanced economic development and integration. EIB loans can be supported by guarantees provided from the European Investment Fund, a pool of money made available by EU Member States, not to be spent on projects directly, but to provide security for the loans without requiring, for example, a charge over assets.

14. An important part of the tender information issued to the prospective promoters was the minimum requirements, which now form a key component of the contract with LCR. They set out the standards and minimum technical specification to which the Link must be designed, and meeting them is a precondition to the opening of the railway. The minimum requirements also specify environmental standards which the Link must meet.

15. In July 1994, four of the consortia: Eurorail CTRL, Green Arrow, LCR and Union Link, were invited to tender for the project. Full bids were submitted in March 1995. After evaluation of the bids in accordance with the published criteria, Eurorail CTRL and LCR were invited to proceed to the final stage of the competition.

The final choice

16. Eurorail CTRL and LCR entered into negotiations with the Department over the specific terms of the contract. They carried out further work on their bids, including a due diligence process to satisfy themselves of the value of the assets they would acquire and further reviews of estimated passenger numbers. They also responded to changes proposed by the Select Committee of the House of Commons, which was considering the Hybrid Bill.

17. In December 1995, these two consortia submitted their final bids for the project reflecting the negotiations and further work. Two months later, LCR was awarded the concession as the selected private sector promoter, having best met the Government's criteria. LCR signed the contract which underpinned the design, construction, finance and maintenance of the link and the operation of Eurostar UK services with the Government on 29 February 1996. This contract, formally known as the Development Agreement, is one of a number of agreements that were signed between the parties over a myriad of issues ranging from changes in circumstances to land provisions. Under the Development Agreement, LCR was obliged to build the Link to minimum performance standards and in return would receive grants from the Government. The grant payments were to be linked to construction performance, with a proportion held back until completion and compliance with the minimum standards agreed. At the time, it was expected that construction would start in 1998 and that the Link would open in 2003.

Eurostar UK regional services

18. Section 40 of the Channel Tunnel Act 1987 required British Rail to prepare plans for the provision or improvement of international rail services to and from various parts of the UK. In December 1989, British Rail announced plans for sleeper international services beginning in Glasgow, Edinburgh, Swansea and Plymouth and daytime international services originating in Manchester, Wolverhampton, Edinburgh and Leeds. British Rail considered that such services would prove profitable.

Sleeper international services

19. As a result, a total of 139 vehicles for overnight rolling stock were ordered in late 1991 by European Night Services Limited (ENS), a cross-border joint venture company in which European Passenger Services Limited (now Eurostar

UK) had a 61 per cent share. The other 39 per cent was divided between France, Germany and the Netherlands. The contract was worth £180 million and was placed with GEC Alstom Metro-Cammell (now Alstom Transport Limited). It was funded through a lease-purchase facility arranged with two UK banks and included a Government guarantee for ENS's share of the contract.

20. Night services did not, however, form part of the minimum requirement for the Link and it was left to bidders to decide on the appropriate level of night services to provide. By 1997, it had become clear to ENS that there was insufficient demand for overnight services to Europe. A global review of night services had also shown that there was not a profitable sleeper service in operation anywhere in the world. At around the same time, Alstom informed ENS that as a result of changes in the specification of the night rolling stock, the cost of completing the contract would increase by at least £100 million. In view of the expected low demand for an overnight Eurostar UK service, ENS concluded that it would not be good value for money to fund the additional cost and the lease arrangements were terminated in February 1998.

21. Because of Eurostar UK's on-going financial difficulties, ENS did not have sufficient funds to finance its share of the termination costs. If the Government's guarantee had not been called, the banks could have forced Eurostar UK into insolvency leading to the collapse of the Link project, which Ministers were at the same time trying to save. The Government therefore allowed the guarantee to be called. This resulted in the Department making payments to the banks totalling almost £109.5 million in June 1998. Provision was made, however, for the Department to recover some of the money if the rolling stock was resold by Alstom. Following negotiations, it was agreed that any profits from sales in excess of £14 million would be shared equally between the Department and Alstom. In addition, there is a counter indemnity in place from Eurostar UK so that the Department can recover the £109.5 million cost of the guarantee and accrued interest if Eurostar UK generates positive cashflows in the future. In January 2001, Alstom announced the sale of the rolling stock to a Canadian rail company for £13.8 million, just below the £14 million threshold for profit sharing with the Department.

Daytime international services

22. In 1991 seven Regional Eurostar train sets for daytime international services were ordered at a cost of £180 million by European Passenger Services Limited. Although the necessary train paths along the East and West Coast Main Lines have been secured, the Regional train sets have never been used for that purpose.

23. Regional Eurostar feeder services began operation in May 1995 with a daily service from Manchester at 07.37 and one from Edinburgh at 08.30. These services were available only to international passengers connecting at Waterloo. Although the fares added only £10-£20 to the cost of the inter-capital fare, the services were not well patronised, attracting only 30-40 passengers each way daily and were withdrawn in 1997.

24. In 1998, ICRR was appointed to take over day to day management of Eurostar UK and to report on the viability of Regional Eurostar services. Its report, delivered in November 1998, supported Eurostar UK's view that such services were not commercially viable. In 2000, the British Railways Board reviewed its plan for international regional services as it was obliged under Section 40 of the Channel Tunnel Act 1987 to keep the plan up to date. This review concluded that Regional Eurostar services would be heavily loss making and that there were no economic, environmental or social grounds for providing a public subsidy.

25. The Government gave permission for Eurostar UK to lease three Regional Eurostar train sets to Great North Eastern Railway for use on the East Coast Main Line. This makes use of currently unused assets and provides much needed extra capacity on the East Coast Main Line, thereby benefiting regional passengers wishing to travel to London and beyond. The deal is short-term and therefore does not prevent the introduction of a Regional Eurostar service in the future. In the meantime, the remaining four train sets are housed in a depot in west London.

The restructured deal: construction of Section 1 of the Link

26. As part of the restructured deal, LCR created two new 100 per cent owned subsidiaries, Union Railways (South) to design and build Section 1 of the Link and Union Railways (North) to build Section 2. LCR had originally contracted Rail Link Engineering (RLE) for the project management, design and construction of the Link. RLE is an unincorporated joint venture led by Bechtel, together with Ove Arup, Sir William Halcrow and Systra. Union Railways has entered into an agreement with RLE so that RLE will continue to project manage the construction of Section 1 of the Link. Upon completion of Section 1, Railtrack will purchase a lease over the infrastructure and related lands until 29 July 2086 (the date on which the Eurotunnel concession terminates). The design and project management of Section 2 remains with LCR as the contract for this work between Union Railways (North) and RLE is awaiting final agreement.

27. Section 1 of the Link will be some 43 miles of twin track high speed overhead electrified railway from the Channel Tunnel to Fawkham Junction. From its connection to Eurotunnel's track at the Channel Tunnel, Section 1 will head west to Ashford and then north west to Southfleet. A two mile spur will run form Southfleet to Fawkham Junction where it will join the existing track leading to Waterloo International. Key works on Section 1 include connections with Ashford International station, a two mile tunnel through the North Downs and a major bridge over the river Medway. The target cost estimate for Section 1 is £1,700 million with a target construction period of 5 years. Construction began in October 1998 and is scheduled to be complete in October 2003.

28. Although Union Railways (South) is a subsidiary of LCR, Railtrack has the obligation to buy Section 1 at a price directly related to the construction cost and is therefore taking the construction risk. As risk taker, Railtrack can make all decisions involving the operations of Union Railways (South) through a right to appoint the directors of the company and approve any payments made. Railtrack also holds a redeemable special share in Union Railways (South).

29. Land acquisition for Section 1 has been carried out by Union Railways (South) as agent of the Secretary of State, using powers granted under the Channel Tunnel Rail Link Act 1996. Acquisition of land for both Sections of the Link must be completed before these powers expire in December 2001. All land acquired is owned freehold by the Government, reflecting the time-limited nature of LCR's interest and the Government's need to protect its long-term ability to continue Eurostar UK operations if the Development Agreement is terminated. There was a considerable amount of surplus land, comprising individual properties acquired for old routes or because they are seriously affected by construction activity. Most of the former have now been sold while the bulk of the latter will be held over until construction is complete and then sold.

30. More substantial areas of land granted to LCR as part of the original deal, mainly at King's Cross and Stratford, offer substantial development opportunities. The Department will receive a half share of any development surplus at these major sites after the cost of bringing the land to development has been deducted. Railtrack has an option to buy into LCR's land development opportunities through an option agreement under the restructured deal.

The restructured deal: Section 2

31. Section 2 of the Link will be 24 miles long. From Southfleet, the planned route will head north west to a new station at Ebbsfleet and then under the Thames estuary through a one-mile tunnel. The route will then continue overland to Dagenham, under East London through a 12-mile tunnel via a new station at Stratford and terminate at St. Pancras. The target cost estimate for Section 2 is approximately £2,500 million with a target construction period of 5½ years. Construction is expected to begin in July 2001 and is scheduled to be complete in December 2006.

The restructured deal: Government grants

32. Government grants for Section 1 are payable on the achievement of set milestones and take two forms. The Capital Grant for construction of the Link is £561 million and is payable in eight instalments. The first installment is payable on the last of a) 15 November 2001, b) achievement of 68 per cent of the target construction cost and c) construction progress reaching the start of secondary tunnel lining. The other instalments are payable quarterly.

33. In addition to the Capital Grant, the Government will also pay a Domestic Capacity Charge to Railtrack for the use of the Link by domestic train services. The charge totals £203 million for Section 1 and is payable in 34 instalments. The first installment will be paid on 18 August 2005 or issue of permit to use, whichever is later.

34. Grants for Section 2 of the Link are on a similar basis to those for Section 1 and amount to £1,058 million (capital) and £192 million (domestic capacity charge).

The restructured deal: operation of the Link

35. Once Railtrack has purchased Section 1, it must provide Eurostar UK with access to the track and stations. Eurostar UK will be entitled to four passenger train paths an hour in each direction and to six train paths an hour when the entire Link is complete. Detailed conditions have also been agreed covering service intervals, stopping patterns and journey times. Eurostar UK will pay access charges to Railtrack for its use of the Link, made up of a number of components:

    a) a fixed track charge designed to provide Railtrack with a return on its investment;

    b) operational and maintenance charges (to be reviewed every ten years);

    c) traction electricity charges (similar to those charged to domestic train operators);

    d) rates based on an expected value to December 2010 (subject to review every five years); and

    e) land rentals from 2030[18].

36. Railtrack will also be obliged to make the Link available to domestic train services. At peak hours, provision has to be made for the operation of 8 services an hour in each direction, reducing to 4 services an hour at other times.

The restructured deal: Economic Benefit Agreement

37. Apart from the sharing of any construction cost underrun on Section 1, Railtrack has agreed that the Department will share in certain exceptional gains, as follows:

    a) In the event that Railtrack sells the subsidiary company it created to operate the Link, up to 75 per cent of any gain on the disposal will be paid to the Department;

    b) The Department will receive a 15 per cent share of any gain (over the purchase price of Section 1) on any off-balance sheet, non-recourse securitised bond issue prior to 2015 which is secured on the fixed charge element of the access charges payable by Eurostar UK to Railtrack.

The restructured deal: termination provisions

38. There are a number of events of default which would entitle the Government to terminate the Development Agreement, including:

    a) a call under one of the Government guarantees;

    b) Eurostar UK annual and cumulative operating cashflows for two successive years falling below the Government Downside Case;

    c) Cumulative access charge loans to LCR exceeding £360 million.

39. On an event of default, the Eurostar UK service would revert to Government ownership. However, the management agreement with ICRR and agreements relating to construction of Section 2 would remain in place.

---

18   *These land rentals are then paid by Railtrack to the Government, which retains the freehold of the land used by the Link.*

Appendix 4 Advisers for the restructuring of the project

A large number of advisers were involved in the restructuring of the project, the major parties involved are listed below.

Advisers to the Department:

J Henry Schroder & Company Ltd (now Schroder Salomon Smith Barney)	Financial adviser
CMS Cameron McKenna	Legal adviser (commercial arrangements)
Linklaters & Paines	Legal adviser (European Commission)
Mott Parsons Gibb	Technical adviser and project representative
Booze-Allen & Hamilton	Eurostar UK revenue adviser
Deloitte & Touche	Accounting and tax adviser
AON	Insurance adviser

Note: The total costs of advice to the Department of negotiating the original and restructured deals, along with monitoring of progress on the project, amounted to some £33 million.

Advisers to LCR:

Deutsche Bank and SBC Warburg Dillon Read	Joint financial advisers
Herbert Smith	Legal adviser
Clifford Chance	Legal adviser to GGB arrangers
Lovell White Durant	Legal adviser to Bechtel
Ashurst Morris Crisp	Legal adviser to National Express
Nabarro Nathanson	Legal adviser to London Electricity
SBC Warburg Dillon Read and HSBC	Joint GGB arrangers
PriceWaterhouseCoopers	Financial modelling
L.E.K. Consulting	Eurostar UK revenue adviser
Ernst & Young	Tax advisers

Advisers to Railtrack:

N M Rothschild & Sons Limited	Financial adviser
Simmons & Simmons	Legal adviser
W S Atkins	Technical adviser
Deloitte & Touche (separate team to that which advised the Department)	Accounting and tax adviser
AON	Insurance adviser

Advisers to ICRR:

Denton Wilde Sapte and Ashurst Morris Crisp	Legal advisers

Appendix 5

Evaluation of funding of London & Continental Railways by RBC Dominion Securities

This report was commissioned by the National Audit Office in relation to certain aspects of the funding of the channel tunnel rail link. This report is for the exclusive use of the National Audit Office and may not be further distributed or reproduced in whole or in part without our written permission.

The views and opinions expressed in this report are confined to the brief set by the National Audit Office and are based on the information made available to us at the time. All views and opinions contained herein constitute our judgement at the time of market conditions and commercial terms prevailing towards the end of 1998 and the first quarter of 1999 and were provided in good faith. We have no duty or liability to any other party other than the National Audit Office, in relation to the views and opinions expressed in this document and in particular the report is not, and should not be construed as, investment advice or an investment advertisement as defined by the Financial Services Act 1986. We expressly disclaim any and all liability for any representation, express or implied, in relation to the securities and transactions discussed herein.

RBC Dominion Securities

JUNE 2000

Summary conclusions

Bank debt

- In our view, the decision to fund the Link through the bond market rather than the bank market was correct on the bases of price, maturity and capacity. The only material advantage of bank debt may have been flexibility. However, this additional flexibility in terms of drawdown schedule and early repayment would probably have been limited by the necessity to hedge future movements in interest rates.

- The bonds were issued on a substantially sub-LIBOR basis, which would not have been achievable in the bank market.

Bond issues

- The Government-guaranteed bonds (GGBs) were launched around the time when the long gilt market was at its highest (in price) for the 12 months around February 1999.

- The spreads on the GGBs were narrower than any other comparable AAA/Aaa Eurobond being issued around that time, and despite strong arguments from investors that they should have been wider.

- The launch of the GGBs was a success. Management of the market (previously critical of the process) improved significantly following a move away from the option of auctioning the bonds.

- In our view, structuring the GGBs as a quasi- or hypothecated Gilt would have achieved a tighter spread (though still a spread premium to the main Gilt market). However, it would not have been possible to structure an issue eligible for the FTSE Gilt Index but still off balance sheet for the Government.

- If the bonds had been quasi-gilts, it is possible that more of the 2038 date bond could have been sold, possibly improving the economics of the project.

- We consider that the book building process was the best route to follow in terms of stimulating competitive interest in the bonds, monitoring the progress of the placing and managing the Gilt market. It was also the cheapest viable route in terms of fees.

Swaps

- The hedging strategy adopted by LCR achieved the objectives of a specific mandate to mitigate exposure to interest rates, given:

  a) the net swap profile required for the anticipated residual cash profile in the Central Case;

  b) the absence of any views on rates other than implied by the yield curve at the time;

  c) the assumption of equal probability of a fall in floating rates as a rise;

  d) the products used would be limited to vanilla swaps without up-front premia;

  e) the selection of a maximum 2011 maturity on the swaps.

- Execution of the hedging strategy by two banks who had prior knowledge of the transaction does not appear to have limited competitive pressure.

- We believe the swap banks were put at risk of losing substantial sums during this process.

- Funding through the Floating Rate Note market may have simplified the hedging process but the additional cost of such bond issues could have been greater than any savings on the hedge.

Bank Debt

The Euroloan markets

1. The Asian crisis in late 1997 jolted the Euroloan market. Interest margins began to rise and maturities began to fall. The Russian crisis of 1998 dealt a further and more serious blow causing total Euroloan market volume to fall from US$459 billion equivalent in 1997 to US$397 billion equivalent in 1998. Emerging market economies suffered the most but Western Europe did not escape. Western European loan volume fell from US$311 billion equivalent in 1997 to US$270 billion equivalent in 1998 whilst maturities shortened and margins rose, even for good quality borrowers. Volume for United Kingdom borrowers fell from US$166.5 billion equivalent to US$138.8 billion equivalent but rose to 36 per cent of the total market (**Figure 21**).

21 | **Loans by borrower nationality: all Euromarket 1998**

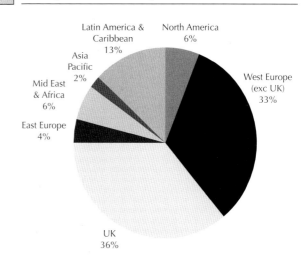

Source: Capital DATA Ltd

General conditions

2. The Euroloan market is priced at a margin (the profit on the transaction) over the relevant inter-bank offered rate, e.g. LIBOR, EURIBOR. The inter-bank offered rate is that at which banks lend to each other in the deposit market and in theory the rate at which banks fund their loan portfolios. The stronger banks fund below that rate through a combination of customer deposits and alternative fund raising methods.

3. As a United Kingdom domiciled borrower, fund raising by LCR in the Euro-loan market would be in the context of prevailing conditions in the Western European sector and the United Kingdom sector in particular. A brief analysis of the type of borrower, the business and industries, and the loan purpose in these two geographies is worthwhile.

4. The majority of borrowers in Western Europe are private, accounting for 88.9% of volume in 1997 and 93.5% in 1998. In the United Kingdom, almost all borrowers are private sector/corporates, project finance and PFI (**Figure 22**). The lack of sovereign/state agency borrowers is not a reflection of the lack of appetite amongst lenders for this sector but a reflection of the cheaper, alternative funding sources available to these borrowers.

5. A further analysis of the Western European and United Kingdom geographies by business type reinforces the commercial private sector nature of the typical borrower with the state sector taking almost no part (**Figures 23 and 24**).

22 **Loans by borrower type: Western Europe 1998**

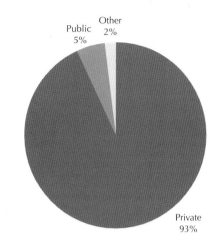

Source: Capital DATA Ltd

23 **Loans by business type: Western Europe 1998**

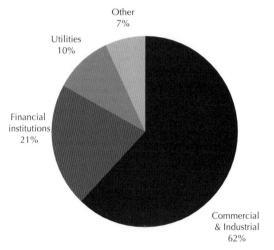

Source: Capital DATA Ltd

24 **Loans by business type: UK borrowers 1998**

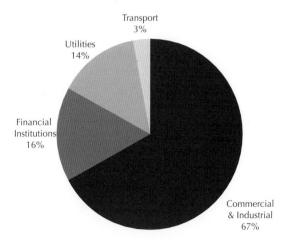

Source: Capital DATA Ltd

6. During 1998, acquisition-related facilities grew from US$89.7 billion equivalent to US$107 billion equivalent. Project financing volume edged up slightly from US$19.2 billion equivalent to US$19.9 billion equivalent in 1997 and 1998, reflecting the continued appetite amongst lenders for structured, higher margin assets **(Figure 25)**. This trend was reflected in the United Kingdom, where project financing rose from US$7.2 billion equivalent in 1997 to US$11.6 billion equivalent in 1998. Despite this increase, and the decline in overall volume, project financing as a percentage of borrowings in the United Kingdom only increased from 5% of total to 7% **(Figure 26)**.

25 **Loans by purpose: Western Europe 1998**

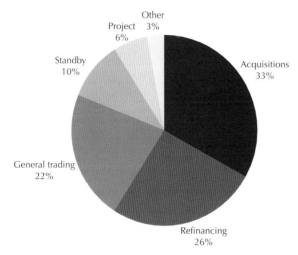

Source: Capital DATA Ltd

26 **Loans by purpose: UK borrowers 1998**

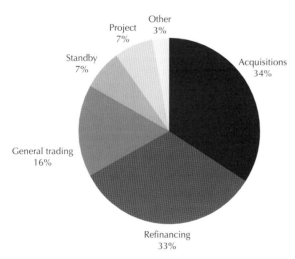

Source: Capital DATA Ltd

7. Across the market as a whole, maturities of less than 5 years increased in proportion to the total volume. The trend was less marked in the stronger economies of Western Europe, and the exception to the rule was the United Kingdom where the proportion of under 5 year maturities fell slightly, along with the virtual demise of the 7-10 year maturity. The changes are shown in **Figure 27** below.

27 **Maturity trends in the Euroloans market 1997 and 1998**

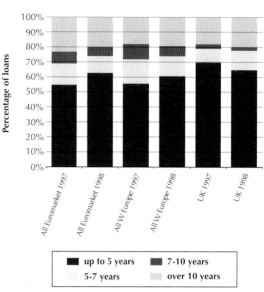

Source: Capital DATA Ltd

8. Average pricing in the Euro-loan market has risen in general since the middle of 1997 but the withdrawal and in some cases, exclusion, of many emerging market borrowers during 1997 and 1998 who traditionally borrowed at higher rates disguises the steep rise seen in margins paid by those still active. The sudden pick up in pricing can be clearly seen in the averages for all Western European and all United Kingdom borrowers and is a truer reflection of the market. By the end of 1998, average corporate pricing had risen by almost 65% from a low point in the middle of 1997 **(Figure 28)**.

28 **Pricing trends in the Euroloans market 1997 and 1998**

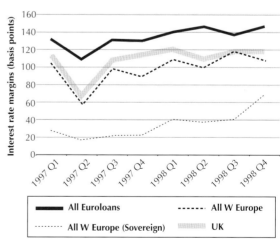

Source: Capital DATA Ltd

Specific considerations

9. Lenders take into account a number of factors when assessing a loan. These include: maturity, credit standing, return (margin and fees), purpose, default probability and opportunities in the primary and secondary loan markets as well as alternative investments in the bond and derivative markets ("benchmarking"). The primary market is well documented and lenders are able to assess alternative opportunities with relative ease. The secondary market is less transparent and until mid-1997 there was no regular forum for tracking yields on secondary market loans, unlike in the bond market.

Primary loan market benchmarks

10. The Euro-loan market began 1999 slowly, during January Western European market volume amounted to only US$ 9.2 billion (US$110 billion annualised) and United Kingdom volume was only US$ 4.2 billion (US$50.4 billion annualised). By the end of February, the volumes were Western Europe US$29.2 billion (US$174 billion annualised) and United Kingdom US$11 billion (US$66.15 billion annualised).

11. Loans launched during the first two months of 1999 would have used facilities concluded in 1998 and any launched in 1999 as benchmarks. Annex 1 shows selected loans signed between January 1997 and March 1999. These cover a wide range of borrowers including pure sovereigns, public bodies/state agencies and major corporates in a range of industries including telecommunications, roads, railways, power generation, healthcare, mining and services.

12. Maturities vary from very short-term to long-term (circa 20 years) for project financing/PFI but there are few transactions over 10 years. Transaction sizes vary but there are few large facilities. It is worth noting that in 1998 there were only 28 transactions greater than £1,000 million equivalent amount for Western European borrowers (mostly acquisition facilities) of which 19 were for United Kingdom borrowers.

13. There are a number of large project financing/PFI facilities that can be used as benchmarks for a non-state supported facility. These include ISAB Energy (approx £580 million), Saltend Co-generation (£718 million), Sarlux (approx £600 million), and a larger number of much smaller facilities e.g. Tagus Bridge, and the United Kingdom transactions for, inter alia, Severn River Crossing and Autolink Concessionaires. These facilities were priced at substantial margins, many in excess of 100 basis points but they did have maturities of the length required.

14. There are several comparable facilities for state-owned or state-supported entities in 1997 and early 1998, but hardly any in late 1998. These include: Aeroports de Paris; Reseau Ferre de France; Charbonnages de France; Radiotelevision Italiana; Posten Norge; Electricidade de Portugal; Ente Publico Radio Television Madrid; and Red Nacional de Ferroccarrilles (RENFE).

15. These transactions were all aggressively priced at their launch but were successful due to risk quality and lender appetite. There were no comparable transactions during the first two months of 1999. However, by the end of 1998, margins had risen substantially from the levels seen in 1997 and there is no doubt that if these transactions had been launched into the market in January or February 1999 the borrowers would have had to pay a higher margin. There are few pure sovereign facilities. Only HM the Queen in Right of Canada and the Kingdom of Spain are equivalent benchmarks, whilst there are a handful of Hellenic Republic transactions which are not equivalent benchmarks.

Secondary loan market benchmarks

16. Secondary pricing tends to be higher than primary pricing for a number of reasons including: there is less or no relationship pressure to buy in the secondary market thus borrowers cannot drive a harder bargain; the distressed state of the Far Eastern banks and their desire to reduce assets led to substantial discounting of loan assets; lead arrangers of transactions have a far larger front end fee than the lower level lenders and can use a part of this to subsidise further sell-down of positions and achieve enhanced returns on their final hold.

17. Annex 2 is a schedule showing the indicative secondary market yields for a number of facilities that would have been used as a benchmark for a facility for LCR launched in the first two months of 1999. The government guaranteed or partially supported facilities had a yield around their margin. Also quoted are indicative yields for the Railtrack facility, which had an average premium of 34% to its original margin. It is worth noting that the remaining maturities for all these transactions are considerably shorter than those LCR required.

Efforts made to seek loan market opportunities

18. Our review of the information made available to us does not reveal that there were extensive efforts made to seek loan market opportunities. There is an apparently unsolicited offer for a financing of £2,000 million from Deutsche Bank AG in June 1998 at pricing and with maturities that we consider would have been appropriate. It is also our view that there was sufficient capacity in the market to raise this finance on the terms proposed.

Railtrack guaranteed loan for LCR

19. LCR raised £700 million through three facilities guaranteed by Railtrack of which £350 million was provided by banks. The terms of this latter facility paying a margin of 45 basis points over LIBOR for the first five years and 55 basis points over LIBOR for the last two years are, in our opinion appropriate for the facility in market at that time.

Conclusion and answers to specific questions raised by the NAO

20. The NAO asked a number of specific questions in the Terms of Reference for the Appointment of Financial Consultants. These questions and the answers are set out below. The answers are based upon a review of the Euro-loan market leading up to February 1999 and the conditions prevailing in the market at that time. The answers to all the questions are, to a greater or lesser extent, linked.

Q   Would it have been feasible to raise bank finance to fund the Link either with or without a Government guarantee?

A   It would certainly have been feasible to raise bank finance with a Government guarantee. We do not believe that sufficient amounts could have been raised without a Government guarantee.

Q   Would there have been sufficient appetite and capacity in the banking market to provide the funding package?

A   There would have been sufficient appetite and capacity to raise up to £2,000 million with a Government guarantee. We do not believe there would have been sufficient appetite and capacity to raise large sums without a Government guarantee or some tangible government support unless LCR paid a substantial (in excess of 1%) margin. Even with a substantial margin, we do not believe it would have been possible to raise all the financing required from the loan market and estimate that £1,000 million in addition to the £350 million Railtrack guaranteed facility would have been the maximum amount available.

Q   What length of financing terms would have been available?

A   A Government guaranteed facility or one with some tangible government support would have been able to obtain a maturity of 12 years and there may have been a requirement for some amortisation in the later years. A facility without a government guarantee would have been limited to 7 years, as in fact was the case for LCR's £350 million facility guaranteed by Railtrack signed in December 1998.

Q   What additional flexibility in the draw-down profile would have been possible?

A   The loan market has a distinct advantage over others in that facilities with a fully revolving draw-down period throughout their life are available. For a project financing, it is possible to structure term loan facilities with extended draw-down periods and the ability to draw in flexible amounts. There would have been greater flexibility in the draw-down schedule in a loan facility than in the bond financings.

Q   What total savings would bank finance have realised for the borrower, LCR, over bond finance?

A   We do not believe that bank finance would have achieved any savings for the borrower over bond finance since loan finance would have been at a margin over LIBOR and the bond issues achieved sub-LIBOR funding. If the loan route had been chosen, in addition to the high interest cost on drawn amounts, LCR would have had to pay a commitment fee on the undrawn (but committed) amounts, thus adding to the overall cost. Although the total bond proceeds were not required at financial close, the excess was put on deposit at a higher rate than the swapped interest cost, creating positive cashflow for LCR.

Q   What would have been the advantages or disadvantages of using bank finance as opposed to, or in conjunction with, bond finance?

A   It can be argued that the £700 million Railtrack guaranteed debt together with the Government-guaranteed bonds does form a dual market financing package. The real question is whether it would have been possible to arrange bank finance in excess of the Railtrack guaranteed debt. There could, for example, have been an initial issue of bonds to refinance existing debt and provide a cash pool for part of the future expenditure. A parallel loan could have been raised at the same time to fund a further part of capital expenditure and the balance of the funding required left until a date in the future. This strategy would have exposed LCR to changes in market conditions which may have affected pricing and maturity available and would also have exposed it to a decline in its own credit quality which may have led to no, or only very expensive finance, being available. Conversely, the opposite could have been the case. On balance, given the history of the Channel Tunnel, Eurostar UK, the high speed rail link, and the more attractive funding available in the bond market in both terms of cost and maturity, arranging almost all the financing required in the bond market resulted in better value and was therefore the more appropriate approach.

The Bond market

Background to issue of Government-guaranteed bonds to fund Section 1 of the Link

21. It appears from the early papers that the original funding structure proposed for LCR involved a combination of debt issues: credit enhanced bonds which would carry the government guarantee, drawings from the European Investment Bank (EIB) and access charge bonds which would benefit from government support but not a guarantee. It seems, therefore, that there was some consideration as to whether the project could issue debt without, or with a limited, explicit guarantee.

22. In June 1998, the Government agreed to provide a series of guarantees to back bonds to be placed into the sterling bond market. Schroders, the Department's financial advisers for the Link, advised that to minimise the cost of these bonds, they needed to be as "Gilt-like" as possible. After consultation with the UK Debt Management Office (DMO) and the market in September and early October, it was agreed that the best way to launch the bonds would be through a book building process. The bonds themselves would be Eurobonds, more like issues by the EIB and Kredietanstalt für Wiederaufbau (KfW) than Gilts.

23. The disruption in the Gilt market in Q4 1998 and the rise in the indicative spread for the GGBs, provoked a review of this decision and in October 1998, the Treasury recommended LCR be funded via an issue of Gilts. This recommendation was rejected, and lead managers experienced in the placing of Eurosterling Bonds were interviewed in November and appointed.

24. It was always accepted that issuing GGBs was likely to create an additional public sector cost, but from the outset it was argued that this could be justified on the following grounds:

   a) the Government guarantee was only a contingent liability and therefore did not form part of the Public Sector funding requirement unlike an issue of Gilts;

   b) the fact that LCR was being funded by the private sector would bring private sector disciplines to the company, protecting the taxpayers' investment;

   c) the project would be seen as a Public Private Partnership.

25. By November 1998, an additional argument was added, that is, that there was insufficient time to restructure the project and obtain EU clearances for direct funding. A complete restructuring would probably have led to the project having to be retendered. The time constraint appears to have been serious as construction had started and LCR was running out of funds. This meant a funding package had to be concluded, despite market conditions.

Market conditions

26. In June 1998 when the agreement to provide a Government guarantee was given, sterling market conditions were reasonably stable, and it was expected that the bonds could be issued at a relatively small premium over Gilts, perhaps similar to that for KfW or EIB. However, the end of Q3 and all of Q4 saw the full brunt of the Russian crisis hit the markets followed by the near failure of LTCM, a major hedge fund. As described below, all bond spreads widened dramatically. The flight to quality drove down Gilt yields.

Margins

27. A general fear in the credit markets caused swap spreads to widen in Q3 1998. This prompted a flood of AAA issuance in Q3-4 1998, as highly rated agencies borrowed in the bond markets and swapped the funds to raise sub-LIBOR funding. **Figure 29** overleaf illustrates the severe widening of credit spreads at the height of the crisis when LTCM was in difficulties and how spreads remained wider into 1999.

29 | European Investment Bank 6% Eurosterling Bonds 2028, interest rate margin over 6% Treasury Stock 2028

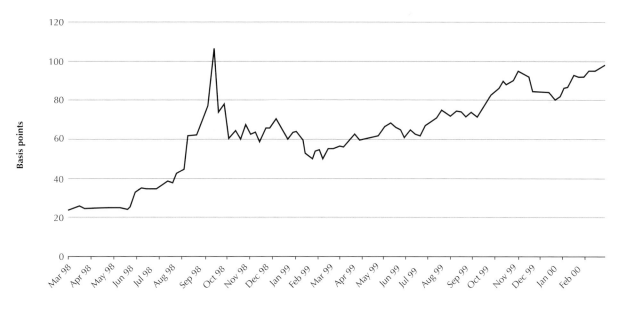

Source: Capital DATA Ltd

28. Given the disrupted market conditions when the decision to issue the GGBs was taken, it was reasonable to argue that only the highest quality bonds would have been bought by investors in large volume.

Volumes

29. **Figure 30** below shows that in the last quarter of 1998 almost 75% of the new issues were for AAA names, and 90% for AAA and AA names. This compares with the first half of the year where AAA fixed rate issuance was less than 50% of the total.

30 | New fixed-rate sterling issues: investment ratings

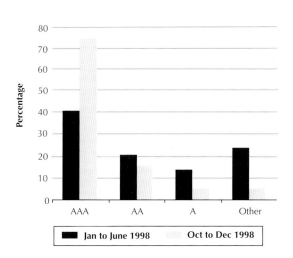

Source: RBC Dominion Securities

30. It is highly unlikely that in Q4 1998 or Q1 1999 any large issue (over £500 million) could have been launched at an aggressive price without a AAA credit rating. Indeed, even in calm market conditions it is difficult to launch very large amounts of bonds into a single part of the yield curve. **Figure 31** below shows a distribution of tranche sizes in the sterling market (fixed rate and floating rates) since 1997. It is clear that issues in excess of £500 million are rare.

31 | Sterling bond issues since 1997

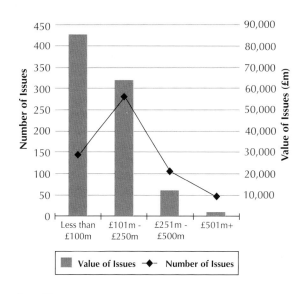

Source: IRF

31. Two other large sales of UK Government assets to the private sector had been funded in the bond market in the last few years, with funding taking place on a single day. These were Annington Homes which launched over £900m of AAA-rated bonds in three different tranches to fund the purchase of MOD Married Quarters Estate and FRESH, the vehicle used to purchase the Housing Corporation Loan Portfolio. FRESH raised over £1,000 million of bonds on one day in 8 tranches, the largest of which were AAA-rated. Both Annington Homes and FRESH were launched into comparatively benign market conditions.

Could the bonds have been issued without the Government Guarantee?

Appetite for project risk

32. There is very little capacity in the sterling market for unrated or non-investment grade rated bonds. It is, therefore, necessary to obtain a credit rating to issue a large amount of fixed rate debt. Figure 30 above illustrates how little non-rated or non-investment grade debt is issued in sterling. (Indeed, most of this is categorised as "High Yield" debt and is generally placed into a separate class of specialist investors.)

33. Project finance is still a novel concept in the sterling bond market and investors are highly reliant on credit rating. Their sensitivity is such that, in sterling, there is currently a preference to buy project finance bonds which have been insured by a specialist credit insurer ("Monoline Insurer") and carry a AAA guarantee. This is the case even if the underlying project has a reasonable investment grade credit rating. **Figure 32** below illustrates that investors may demand a margin of some 70 basis points additional return for an A-rated project. At the time LCR launched its bonds this yield difference was wider.

34. Given the history of the project, it seems that it was unlikely to achieve an investment grade rating without a substantial injection of equity and support from creditworthy sponsors or Government.

35. Some of the prime areas where the rating agencies would have been nervous would be:

a) unpredictability of operating cashflow;

b) basis risk. LCR's income would be a mixture of floating rate interest income, fixed/variable rate purchase proceeds from Railtrack, (RPI linked) grants and RPI correlated income from Eurostar UK. Its commitments would not necessarily match;

c) contingency of Section 2 of the Link;

d) repayment of 2010 bonds partly dependent on Railtrack Group plc guarantee. This is unrated but can be assumed to be A-rated (i.e. a notch lower than the regulated utility, Railtrack PLC). This might act as a cap to the rating;

e) rating agencies are sensitive to construction risk in major projects;

f) the nature of any Government support.

36. It seems that the Government was also constrained by a) a need to change the original concession to LCR as little as possible and b) time, as LCR was running out of money. Given the nature of this project and these constraints, we do not believe that it would have been possible to achieve a high enough rating to attract sufficient demand for bonds issued by LCR without substantial Government support.

32 **Credit margins of un-enhanced over enhanced bonds**

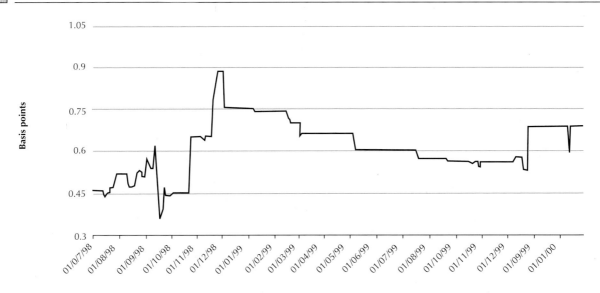

Source: RBC Dominion Securities

37. The Government Guarantee, therefore, brought a number of benefits to the funding process:

    a) it removed credit risk;

    b) it enabled the bonds to carry a low risk weighting;

    c) it enabled the bonds to carry explicit AAA/Aaa credit rating;

    d) it enabled the bonds to be simply structured without a complex repayment schedule;

    e) it enabled a large amount of bonds to be sold at one time, especially in disrupted markets;

    f) it allowed longer tenors to be issued.

38. However, the use of the Guarantee could not:

    a) turn the issue into a Gilt;

    b) remove the illiquidity premium;

    c) remove market and performance risk;

    d) avoid some consequential activity in the Gilt market.

39. There is a strong argument in favour of the Government guarantee as the only way of issuing the bonds in large volume and in disrupted market conditions. The question is whether the guarantee enabled LCR to issue the bonds on the cheapest possible basis.

Pricing of the Government-guaranteed bonds

Cost differential between AAA-rated debt

40. The Government's advisers clearly identified that the cost to the public sector of providing a guarantee was not the net present value of the risk margin on the bonds above Gilts. Rather, the cost was the amount of other support Government had to provide to LCR as a result of higher funding costs (e.g. in access charge loan facilities) and, in extremis, the cost of any calls on the guarantee.

41. The extent of these costs and their degree of contingency were dependent on LCR meeting or improving on the Department's base case projections. We understand that extensive stochastic analysis had been carried out on the traffic forecasts and it was concluded that the likelihood of a call on the guarantee was low. Timely payment of the bonds is also dependent on the receipt of purchase proceeds from Railtrack for each section of the Link. The likelihood of Railtrack meeting its obligations should be reflected in its credit rating. Railtrack's gearing is also taken into account by its regulator, who has an interest in the company retaining a sound credit rating and continuing access to the debt markets.

42. It was important, therefore, to minimise LCR's cost of funds in order to keep the secondary government support as low as possible and to minimise the financial risks within LCR. This section illustrates that AAA bonds of identical credit risk do not necessarily trade at the same spread and puts the GGB pricing into the context of other risk-free or very low risk bond yields.

---

33 | **Sterling AAA bond yields**

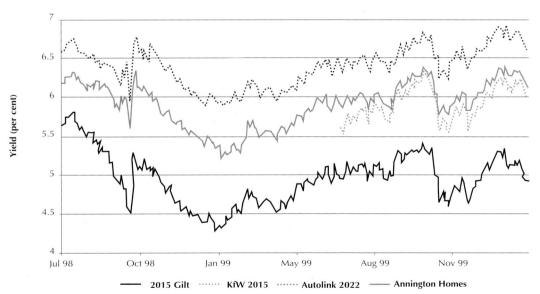

Yield (per cent)

——— **2015 Gilt** ········ **KfW 2015** ········ **Autolink 2022** ——— **Annington Homes**

Source: RBC Dominion Securities

43. Non participants in the market can be shocked by the differential spread between bonds of the same maturity and same credit rating. **Figure 33** shows the yields of three AAA bonds relative to the Gilt. (We have illustrated these bonds because they have a similar weighted average life. There is not a suitable range of AAA bonds at 2028-38 maturities).

44. Although these bonds have the same credit rating there are a number of differences in their structure, eligibility for investment and investors' perception of how each will perform relative to other investments. All of these differences can be said to contribute to the liquidity of the bonds.

Why were the GGBs issued at a margin to Gilts and was this margin minimised?

45. This section considers why the GGBs were issued at a margin to Gilts, whether attempts were made to minimise it and whether the margin was justified. The three bond issues were launched at the following risk margins to Gilts:

Issue-Closing Date	Nominal Amount	Coupon	Issue	Maturity Date	Risk Margin
10-18 Feb 99	£1,225,000,000	4.5%	Guaranteed bonds	2028	+0.33%
10-18 Feb 99	£425,000,000	4.5%	Guaranteed bonds	2038	+0.28%
17-25 Feb 99	£1,000,000,000	4.5%	Guaranteed bonds	2010	+0.375%

46. Tradeable Obligations issued by Central Governments, such as Gilts or US Treasuries, tend to be the most liquid securities in all markets. Schroders, correctly in our view, advised that the GGBs would be sold at the best price if they could be treated as a Gilt. There were a number of features of the GGBs, which inevitably distinguished them from an issue of gilts and resulted in a cost differentiation. Most of these features were unavoidable given the constraints imposed by the structure of the project and time.

47. Annex 3 summarises the pricing of a fixed rate sterling bond. Given that the credit risk on a GGB is the same as that for a Gilt, the additional cost can be explained by illiquidity and performance risk. Features (described in more detail below) which influence these risks include:

- size of issuer;
- universe of investors;
- maturity;
- administration and settlement;
- index eligibility;
- method of sale.

Illiquidity - size of issue

48. The 5 largest Gilt issues in the market at the time the GGBs were issued were:

Name of issue	Size (£bn)
7% Treasury Stock 2001	12.8
7.5% Treasury Stock 2006	11.7
8% Treasury Stock 2015	13.8
8% Treasury Stock 2021	16.5
8% Treasury Stock 2028	11.5

It has been the policy of the DMO to concentrate issuance on a few benchmark issues, some of which may also have special characteristics such as being strippable. Gilts are also subject to the special relationship between the DMO and Gilt Edged Market Makers (GEMMS). Even if a quasi-Gilt, with these privileges had been issued, it can be seen that it would have been too small to trade in line with the major issues in the Gilt market. The Figures in Annex 3 illustrate that small issues of Gilts trade at a discount to the large benchmark issues.

49. Once the decision had been made to issue Eurobonds, it was inevitable that they would be issued at a further spread premium to Gilts. However, would it have been possible to issue the GGBs as a single tranche to obtain greater liquidity? Given the final corporate eurobond structure, we do not believe there would have been sufficient demand for a single £2,650 million tranche. Investors will have more restrictive exposure limits on corporate bonds than Gilts. Therefore, although a small issue will be illiquid and trade at a spread premium, there is also a spread premium for volume. When placing large amounts of bonds on a single day it is therefore necessary to access as many investors as possible and this tends to be achieved by selling the bonds in various maturity tranches (cf. FRESH/Annington Homes). The long GGBs were issued in two tranches reflecting the relative demand for each maturity.

Illiquidity - universe of investors

50. As a general rule, securities which are consistently attractive to a wide variety of investors are the most liquid. It is fair to say that a sovereign Treasury Stock is likely to have the largest universe of potential investors compared with other types of security. Gilts are credit risk free and depending on an investor's time horizon can be seen as cash equivalent. Gilts are eligible investments for most portfolios and even equity fund managers will put surplus cash into the Gilt market or switch out of shares into Gilts when they are nervous of the equity markets. In addition:

- overseas investors will hold Gilts as a risk free exposure to sterling;

- retail investors are substantial buyers of Gilts. Market makers specialising in retail sales of Gilts believe that retail investors may account for up to 10% of Gilt sales;

- corporate investors may keep cash balances in short Gilts or use them to collateralise sinking funds;

- banks - Gilts are used to hedge underwriting positions and as the underlying deliverable instrument in the swaps and derivatives market.

Illiquidity - maturity

51. Certain structural features can make a risk-free security more or less attractive to certain classes of investor. Maturity is one such feature. As for the majority of PFI style infrastructure projects, extending the prepayment schedule of the LCR debt improved its economics. The project's requirement for long dated funding coincided with a shortage of long dated Gilts which fund managers were finding (and continue to find) a hindrance to the efficient management of their long-term liabilities.

52. The 2028 GGBs were structured to imitate a Gilt in terms of maturity by having pay days identical to those of the 6% Treasury Stock 2028. As a result the GGBs can be seen as a Gilt alternative within a portfolio or for use as a bond market hedge. **Figure 34** shows the maturities of sterling bond issues in 1998 and 1999. Some fund managers have a desire for assets with an even longer maturity. This was met by the 2038 issue. From a project net present value point of view, the longer the better. It would seem, however, that demand was fairly limited as the issue is relatively small.

53. Given the appetite for long dated debt, it could be asked why £1,000 million of 2010-dated bonds were issued. As mentioned above, the advantage of issuing a bond in multi-tranche form at different maturities can be that it enables a wider group of investors to be accessed. More importantly, however, the 2010 issue was subject to the swap arrangements discussed later and its redemption coincides with the latest date for receipt from Railtrack of

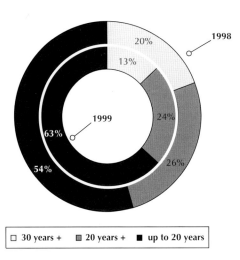

34 | **Maturity of sterling bonds 1998 and 1999**

| □ 30 years + | ■ 20 years + | ■ up to 20 years |

Source: IFR

its purchase consideration for the completed Link. It should be noted that redeeming fixed rate debt before its final maturity can be extremely costly due to penalties payable in certain market conditions. It was therefore a better solution to issue 2010 bonds than issue optically cheaper 2028/2038 bonds and pay penalties for early repayment.

Illiquidity risk - administration and settlement

54. Schroders and the Department appear to have had extensive discussions with the DMO about direct Gilt funding and the possibility of the GGBs being treated as Gilts. The DMO's views were sought in relation to the distribution method of the GGBs and the possibility of an auction (discussed in greater detail below). We understand that although the DMO believed an auction of GGBs would have been technically possible, auction of a product traded at a margin to gilts, would have been complex and a different type of system would probably have had to be put in place. The DMO do not believe any serious thought had been given to how a spread auction would be administered.

35 | **Yields on annuity and bullet issues 1998-1999**

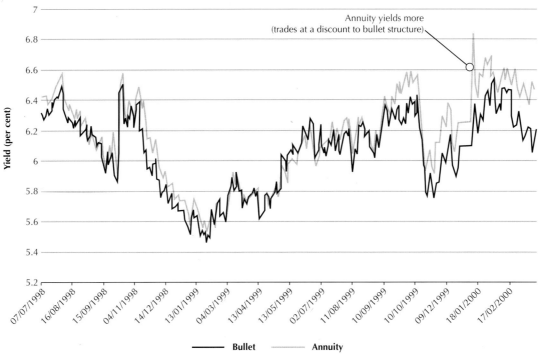

Source: RBC Dominion Securities

Performance risk - index eligibility

55. Many fund managers are benchmarked against the FTSE Gilt indices. If the GGBs were included in the Index, holdings could be benchmarked against it. The FTSE Actuaries Bond Indices Committee rejected the GGBs for inclusion in the Index. To comply with the index requirements would probably have required the bonds to be direct on balance sheet obligations of HM Government. As a consequence of non-inclusion, some investors could not treat the GGBs as Gilts even if they had been identical in every other respect. Instead, they would be treated like other non-Gilt bonds. The GGBs were finally sold at spreads slightly tighter than that of comparable risk-free, but non-Gilt, bonds, such as EIB and KfW. This being the case, some investors declined the GGBs in preference for the likes of EIB from which they could earn a slightly higher yield. We have spoken to major UK pension funds who either did not participate in the transaction or purchased fewer bonds for this reason.

Illiquidity - structural issues

56. Even though the GGBs were not eligible for the Index and enjoyed no DMO privileges, they could still be structured so as to trade as similarly to Gilts as possible. Most Gilts have semi annual coupons and are redeemed in full on a single date ("bullet repayment"). A complex or non conventional bond structure will generally add to the spread. Therefore, if it was the aim to issue the GGBs at the tightest spread achievable, we believe that it was correct to issue the GGBs as a series of fully paid, bullet repayment bonds even if this meant more complex cash management within LCR. AAA rated bonds with complex cashflow schedules, such as annuities, trade at material discounts to bullet repayment bonds (**Figure 35**).

57. One suggestion to ensure the bonds were a quasi Gilt was to make the GGBs convertible into Gilts. This was rejected and in our view would have added a complexity to the bond which would have been detrimental to the pricing. The table below compares the structure of the GGBs with that of a Gilt and another government guaranteed bond for GEFCO, a finance vehicle established by the Export Credits Guarantee Department.

Comparison of Gilt with GGB

	GILT	GEFCO	GGB
Issuer	Usually HM Treasury	GEFCO	LCR Finance plc
Guarantee	Charge on National Loans fund with recourse to consolidated fund of United Kingdom	Secretary of State for Trade and Industry	SoS for Environment, Transport & Regions
Interest	Semi annual in arrear Actual/Actual	Semi annual in arrear A/A	Semi annual in arrear A/A
Repayment	Bullet, callable	Bullet	Bullet
Optional Early Repayment	None	None	Spens
Form	Registered	Registered/Bearer - quoted Eurobond	Quoted Eurobond - Bearer with Registered option
Pricing	Quoted in decimals	Quoted in decimals	Quoted in decimals
Denomination	1p	1p	£1,000
Settlement agent/Registrar	Central Gilts Office (CGO)	CGO + paying agent	Various
Tax call	None	None	None
Tax gross up	None	None	In certain circumstances
Net or gross payments	Gross	Gross to non UK holders	Gross to non UK holders
AAA rating	Implicit	Implicit	Explicit
Repo/strip	Possible on some Gilts	No	No
GEMM privileges	Yes	[yes]	[No]
Sales method	Price auction (nowadays)	Underwritten	Book built
Sales restrictions	None	Standard	Standard + 144(A) option

58. The differences set out in this table seem to be small. Most major investors now find it easier to deal in Eurobonds than in domestic bonds and some attempt appears to have been made to avoid the difficulties of US selling restrictions on Eurobonds by introducing a 144A option.

59. Eurobond form may, however, make the issue less user-friendly for the UK retail investor. Firstly, Eurobonds listed on the London Stock Exchange through the concessionary method of placing, can only be sold initially to professional investors. Secondly, the £1,000 minimum denomination and multiple is high in comparison with Gilts. Lastly, investors can only hold this type of Eurobond if they have a nominee account with access to a Eurobond clearing system. Retail demand for the long issues might have been fairly limited, but there could have been interest for the 2010 issue.

Illiquidity/performance risk - method of Sale

60. The other reason for treating the issue as a Gilt would be the method of sale. It was hoped the GGBs could be sold by auction. This was also rejected by the market. As it was not possible to issue the GGBs as a quasi Gilt, it was issued as a Eurobond. Eurobonds are generally underwritten. However, Schroders rejected proposals for an underwritten issue and followed the book built route.

Would the cost of a quasi Gilt have been cheaper than a Eurobond?

61. There is no example of an instrument which has all the characteristics of a Gilt but was issued to fund a particular project. The only other public bond issues which carry an explicit Government guarantee are those by GEFCO. When the first GEFCO bonds were issued it was the aim of the underwriters to structure them to be as Gilt-like as possible. Although the GEFCO issues are relatively small, when the 2010 issue was first launched in 1989, it was one of the largest single tranche issues in the market. It was launched at around +40 basis points spread to Gilts, and was issued on an underwritten basis. The arguments for the GEFCO spread were:

   a) the bond was a GGB but not a Gilt;

   b) it was implicitly, not explicitly, AAA rated;

   c) a lack of liquidity in comparison with Gilts.

62. GEFCO bonds continue to trade at a discount to Gilts. This feature, that the GGBs trade at a discount to Treasuries, is common to other bond markets. A useful comparison is perhaps the bond issuance of Öresundskonsortiet. This is the vehicle set up to fund the bridge between Sweden and Denmark and its bonds carry explicit guarantees from both the Kingdoms. A SEK1Bn Öresund was issued at 10 years in Swedish Krona this year at SEK Treasuries + 50 basis points. Its bonds trade around these levels in all Scandinavian currencies. In Canada, there are several Crown Agencies which have the same status as Canadian Treasuries in terms of their claim on the Consolidated Fund. They currently trade at spreads of 12 to 15 basis points above Canadian $ Treasuries.

Was book building the cheapest and most appropriate method of distribution?

63. Gilt issues are nowadays issued by price auction. Bidders receive Gilts at the price they bid and the success of a conventional auction is measured by the "Tail" - the range of prices from the average to the lowest price. Eurobonds, sold at a spread to Gilts ("spread product"), are never sold in the UK by auction but are nowadays distributed by underwritten placing or a non-underwritten placing via a book building process. There are other methods of sale but a placing to professional investors allows bonds to be listed on the London Stock Exchange on a concessionary basis with the necessity to publish very limited listing particulars. Both these methods of placing should ensure full placement of bonds.

Auction

64. The conventional auction method was rejected by the market. The auction could not be identical to a Gilt auction as the GGBs are a spread product. The auction would, therefore, have to be a spread auction. Investors in Eurobonds by convention tend to subscribe for an initial placing of bonds all at the same price or spread. The auction would probably, therefore, have had to be an auction where all bidders bought at a single price rather than the type of auction currently used in the conventional Gilt market.

65. Although we believe it would have been technically possible to use an auction, we also believe it would have had certain drawbacks:

- there was an assumption that the auction would be a cheap method of distribution. Gilt auctions are only "cheap" because they are managed by the DMO. The GEMMs are also essential to the process, providing liquidity in the market. There is no reason to believe that the GEMMs would have taken on the sale of the GGBs on the same basis (i.e. for no fee) unless the GGBs had been formally deemed to be Gilts and subject to GEMM privileges;

- generally, institutions put in their bids at auction at the very last minute. If in the case of the GGBs, investors were intending to sell Gilts against their new investment, it would have been much more difficult to manage volatility in the Gilt market;

- in an auction process, it would have been much more difficult to assess how successful the sale would be and the final pricing.

66. LCR might, therefore, have discovered that it had saved fees but paid more on the spread for the bonds.

Underwritten placing

67. Underwritten placings are the most common form of Eurobond distribution. Usually bonds are underwritten after close of business the night before the issue is launched. The underwriter's commitment is to underwrite the bonds at a given spread. The price of the bonds, based on that spread over a reference Gilt, is fixed at an agreed time some hours after the launch is announced.

68. At launch, the underwriter(s) offer the bonds to investors usually at the spread at which they are committed. On pricing, the sale is formalised and the bonds are paid for on the closing date, maybe up to three weeks from launch date. Any unsold bonds are purchased at the issue price by the underwriter. The underwriter is paid a fee which is deducted from the proceeds.

69. For a long dated issue (15 years +), the fee is usually 5/8% of funds raised and ½% at 10 years, although sovereign and supranational issuers of the calibre of EIB can obtain better rates. Via this route, the borrower is guaranteed funds. However, he is exposed to Gilt market risk from the signature of the underwriting agreement to the time the price is fixed, usually only a few hours. To avoid this, a bank will sometimes offer to underwrite a fixed price. In this case, the borrower is transferring market risk to the underwriter who will charge for this. This type of underwriting (a "bought deal") is usually only used for smaller issues, further tranches of existing bonds or arbitrage driven transactions where an associated swap is involved.

Book building

70. Book building is a non-underwritten form of placing. One or several book builders will pre-market a transaction and discover how much each investor will purchase of a bond at a given spread. For example an investor may buy £5m of a bond if the spread is 100 basis points but £7.5m if the spread is 110 basis points.

71. The book builders could be seen as finding the clearing price for the bonds for which they take no risk. However, a well run book building process can stimulate considerable enthusiasm and competitive pressure such that the clearing price improves over time. It has certain other advantages: book building is a marketing process where interest in the bonds is stimulated; a record can be kept of who is participating in the issue; a very detailed picture of the way the distribution process is going is built up over time and it can be adjusted accordingly - there should be no surprises; and fees are usually lower as the book builders' capital is not at risk.

72. Maybe the most important factor for the placing of a very large spread product issue is the management of the underlying Gilt market. As the book builders gradually discover the intentions of their purchasers, they can take steps to manage the flow of bonds into the Gilt market.

73. We believe the appropriate method to distribute the GGBs was book building although there was the risk that the clearing spread would have been wider. Many market participants were talking about wider spreads on the GGBs until very close to launch. This risk was perhaps also illustrated by the relative lack of success of the 2010 issue which was placed at a wider spread. We cannot, however, say that a better price would have been achieved via an underwritten placing; if anything we would be inclined to say that pricing would have been worse. This is partly because the underwriters would have sought to protect themselves against the risk of having to hold unplaced bonds. In addition, investors would have been fearful of poor performance of the stock if there was a chance that underwriters were having to hold large unsold positions.

74. It is difficult to analyse whether the final success of the long dated GGBs was as a result of the enthusiasm built up during the book building process or conditions in the Gilt market conducive to the placement of this type of issue. The more limited success of the 2010 issue illustrates that demand was less where the shortage of Gilts was not so severe.

75. Finally, we believe that the selection of book builders was important. Book builders were selected who are committed to the corporate bond market as well as the Gilt market in the UK. We believe the book builders would have been willing to buy any part of the GGBs still unplaced at the end of the book building process to ensure its success. It was a view in the market that this did in fact happen with the 2010 issue.

Were the fees paid to the book runners in line with the market?

76. A placing of bonds contractually undertaken as a book building process is still rare in the United Kingdom so there is no standard fee basis and little evidence for the outcome of fee negotiations. We should expect fee negotiations to be benchmarked against standard fees for an underwritten placing. The fees paid for the book building process were substantially below those for an underwritten transaction. The published fees on the bonds were as follows:

2028 Bonds:

Selling concession £0.125% on £1.225bn	£1,531,250
Underwriting commission £0.0625% on £1.225bn	£765,625

2038 Bonds:

Selling concession £0.125% on £425m	£531,250
Underwriting commission £0.0625% on £425m	£265,625

2010 Bonds:

Selling concession £0.1% on £1bn	£1,000,000
Underwriting commission £0.05% on £1bn	£500,000

77. This compares well with the fee levels for Eurobonds issued for borrowers such as EIB where the published fees on a large new underwritten bond might be up to £0.45% for a long issue and £0.375% for a medium date. However, fees paid by the highest quality borrowers are generally negotiable and a further substantial discount was negotiated for the book building process, resulting in the actual fees paid being below the published levels quoted above. Given the work and resources involved, reputational risk and support of the issue required, the level of the actual fees paid does not, in our opinion, seem unreasonable.

Issue Date	GGBs	Maturity Date	Risk Margin	Comparators	Maturity Date	Risk Margin
10 Feb 99	LCR	2028	0.33%	EIB	6% 2028	0.49%
10 Feb 99	LCR	2038	0.28%	KfW	6% 2028	0.52%
17 Feb 99	LCR	2010	0.375%	EIB	5½% 2009	0.47%

Investors' perspective

Were the bonds issued on the most favourable terms for investors?

78. Investors want to buy cheap, low risk bonds which remain liquid in the after market. It is the lead managers' job to balance those requirements with those of the issuer. The bonds were launched at a time when there was a great shortage of long dated Gilts and investors were keen to buy Gilt equivalent type assets. The bonds were issued on favourable terms to investors in the sense that they were made as liquid as possible within the constraints already discussed. Depending on the motivation and performance measurement of each investor, the GGBs would either have been viewed as cheap, but illiquid Gilts or expensive AAA Eurobonds, comparable with issues by EIB or KfW.

79. It seems that there were a number of investors, in particular those measured against the FTSE Actuaries Gilt Index, who felt that they could not invest at the final pricing if the GGBs were not in the index. Had they been included, the GGBs would have been cheaper compared with Gilts; but as Eurobonds they were expensive compared with their supposed peer group.

80. Were the bonds targeted at the right type of investors in order to create as much competition in the market as possible? As far as we are aware (we have seen very little written evidence and we would not expect the book runners to reveal this to us), the bonds were offered to a wide range of fixed income investors in the UK and abroad. We have also noted that it appears that some effort was made to sell the bonds into the US at issue. We believe that the lead managers may have succeeded in selling bonds to investors who previously have only bought Gilts and this compensated for the absence of a number of major Eurobond investors. The bonds were not as retail friendly as Gilts but without an expensive marketing exercise we do not think that retail investors would have bought a material number of bonds.

How competitive was the book building process used to price and allocate the bonds?

81. We believe that the book building exercise was successful in stimulating competitive pressure. This is evidenced by the fact that the price talk very close to issue was still wide of bonds issued by KfW and EIB. On the day, LCR bonds were priced inside these AAA comparables as illustrated in the table above.

Were the bonds received well by investors and have they performed well since?

82. We believe that the success of the GGBs has been illustrated above and that the hostile reception given to some of the early proposals regarding distribution method (via an auction) and pricing had no detrimental effect on the outcome of the issues in terms of the launch price. This is important as the success of the launch may influence the performance of the bond in the aftermarket. This in turn acts as a benchmark for further issuance.

83. **Figure 36** overleaf illustrates the performance of the bonds against Gilts in the after market. The widening trend in spread broadly tracks the trend in the sterling swap and AAA corporate bond markets. The 2010 issue appears to have relatively outperformed the others in spread terms. This may in part be due to the fact that swap spreads have tightened at 10 years relative to the long maturities. However, it may also be due to the fact that the 2010 issue was originally placed at a wider spread to compensate investors for the perception that is was the least popular of the three issues.

84. **Figure 37** overleaf illustrates the relative performance of the long LCR bonds to the long EIB bond. If the margin on bond A narrows relative to that on bond B, in relative terms bond A is said to have outperformed bond B as its price has risen more, or fallen less, than bond B's. In this case LCR 38s have outperformed EIB 28s and LCR 28s have very slightly underperformed over the period.

36 **LCR bonds: market performance after issue**

Source: RBC Dominion Securities

37 **Performance of LCR bonds maturing in 2028 and 2038 against European Investment Bank bonds maturing in 2028**

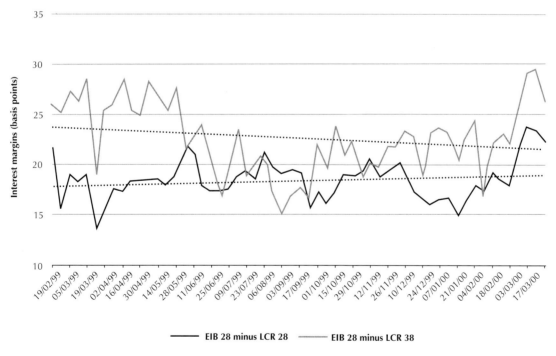

Source: RBC Dominion Securities

How successful was the market management ahead of issue?

What was the strategy?

85. The issue of £2,650 million of bonds on a single day by a single issuer could have been extremely disruptive to the market. Care was taken to ensure that the DMO was informed of the timetable for issuance to ensure that it did not clash with Gilt auctions. However, disruption could still have resulted as it was likely that many investors would sell Gilts in order to release cash to invest in the higher yielding GGBs ("switching"). It was estimated that 30% of purchasers could be switching out of Gilts.

86. Generally investors switching out of Gilts to invest in corporate bonds will conduct this trade at the time the price of the new bond is fixed. This can mean that the Gilt market is disrupted and Gilt prices fall. Investors usually sell the benchmark Gilt against which the bond is priced. As a consequence, the bond is priced with a more expensive coupon. Depending on market conditions, this disruption can occur when a relatively small number of Gilts are sold into the market.

87. The lead managers of the bonds, therefore, advised that a market management strategy be put in place. In summary, this involved selling ("shorting") Gilts before the bond issues were announced and buying them back on pricing of the bonds (from investors who wanted to sell). The strategy was intended to stabilise the Gilt market and it would have protected LCR from an upward movement of the Gilt market just ahead of launch.

88. A "short" is a sale by market participants of a security they do not actually own and the trade can only be settled by buying back the security or delivering borrowed stock. Shorting any security exposes the seller to material risk and it is essential that they can estimate accurately how many securities they should sell and that they can buy them back. When this strategy is combined with an issue of bonds (which it frequently is) the gain or loss on the short trade will be matched by an approximately equal and opposite gain or loss on the price of the bond.

89. The risk was also mitigated by the book building exercise which gave the lead managers an indication of the likely number of gilts to be sold on a switch basis ahead of launch. This knowledge enabled them to manage the market in a more efficient manner. The Government, its advisers and LCR took Counsel's opinion to ensure that this market management exercise was not in breach of the Financial Services Act 1986 nor other securities regulations.

Was the strategy successful?

90. **Figure 38** shows the stability of the Gilt market in the six months around the issue of the LCR bonds. The long end of the market is more volatile than the 10 year area so we should expect any volatility to show up here more clearly.

---

38 Movements in the Gilt market and European Investment Bank bond maturing in 2028

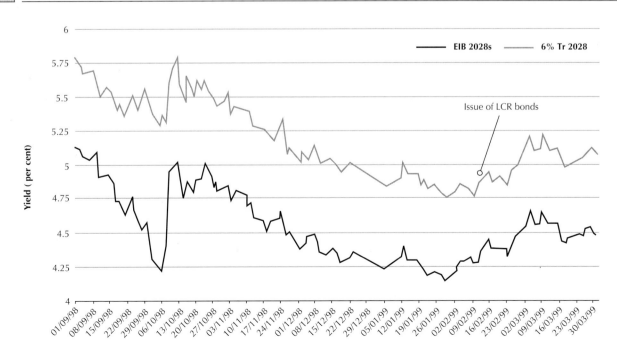

Yield (per cent)

EIB 2028s   6% Tr 2028

Issue of LCR bonds

Source: RBC Dominion Securities

91. The 30 day average volatilities measured as a standard deviation around the mean yield for the quarter around the issue are as follows:

	Q3 1998	Q4 1998	Q1 1999	Q2 1999
6% Tr 2028	13.6%	10.5%	10.6%	13.9%
6% EIB 2028	13.7%*	12.7%	11.7%	14.3%

* 2 months data only

Source: Bloomberg

92. It can be seen from this table that volatility in Q1 1999 was lower than in the months immediately preceding and following it. We believe this was a relatively stable period in the market in comparison to the last 2 quarters of 1998 when the consequence of the hedge fund crisis had a dramatic effect on the Gilt market. Nevertheless, selling over £2,650 million of sterling bonds would have disrupted the market if a market management strategy had not been in place.

93. It is difficult to assess any cost incurred as a result of the hedging strategy. However, it appears that the Government's advisers attempted to verify prices at which trades were dealt and the correspondence we have seen suggests that the lead managers conducted the trades relating to the management strategy away from their Gilt desks to ensure no conflicts arose. Given the fragility of market sentiment in the first quarter of 1999 and the size of the GGB placing, it is our view that the market management strategy reduced the risk of an adverse market movement which could have resulted in the GGBs being issued at a higher interest rate.

What are the prospects for a new issue of LCR bonds?

94. Under the terms of the Development Agreement, LCR must fund the construction of Section 2 of the Link. In order to ensure LCR can meet this commitment, a number of arrangements have been put in place, including the facility for LCR to issue a further £1,100 million of GGBs. These will have a final maturity of no later than 31 December 2010 (which is the last date for Railtrack to purchase the completed Section 2).

95. It is common practice in the Sterling Bond Market to issue further tranches of bonds. A new bond issue can have the same legal status as an existing issue in all respects but form a separate series or it can be part of the same series. A series of bonds is a class of securities where all the terms are identical including the coupon, payment dates and maturity. It is, therefore, impossible after issue to distinguish a new bond from an existing bond of the same series.

96. The main advantage of issuing a new tranche of bonds to be consolidated with an existing issue is that the total issue size is increased and this may, therefore, add to the bonds' liquidity. In theory, a more liquid bond should trade at an improved price. However, the price of this existing bond will act as a guide for pricing the new issue. If further GGBs are issued it would seem logical to create them in the same series as the existing 2010 bonds so they can be consolidated with them. It is, therefore, important that the existing bond is seen to be successful in order to ensure the best price for the new stock.

97. We cannot predict the appetite for a future issue of LCR bonds. However, we can perhaps say that it is unlikely that there would be as much demand for a 2010 issue as for a longer bond. This is in part due to the continuing shortage of Gilts which is exaggerated at the long end of the market. However, this is evaluating the bonds in isolation from the project. Additional 2010 bonds should be repayable from the proceeds of Railtrack's expected purchase of Section 2, reducing the debt in LCR and the overall risk profile of the borrower.

98. We do not wish to labour the relative unattractiveness of the existing 2010 issue. It is highlighted only because of the exceptionally aggressive pricing achieved for the longer dated GGBs. In terms of a comparison with bank debt, even in then current market conditions, a further issue of 2010 bonds would be priced substantially below LIBOR, achieving similar cashflow management benefits to LCR as the existing issue (although a new 2010 issue would, by definition, be less than 10 years and not therefore as attractive as a straight 10 year issue).

The swap market

Market background

99. Volumes in "Over the Counter" derivatives generally slowed in the first half of 1999 as all major financial markets stabilised following significant event risk over both the preceding half year (1998) and also the previous Autumn (1997). Risk-taking positions by market professionals reduced over that period, as well as the use of swap spreads as a "proxy" for credit spread risk mitigation (ie the use of swaps to protect against movements in credit spreads). The swap market in the second half of 1998 had seen unusual and significant use, notably by investment banks and dealers to mitigate their exposures to rising credit spreads. Swap spreads in the second half of 1998 in the major markets had widened dramatically to historic highs, particularly in the 10-year plus sector. During the first half of 1999, swap spreads gradually, but consistently, declined. The mechanics of the swap market are described in Annex 4.

Sterling

100. Sterling swap spreads followed the general market pattern described above. Swap spreads at 10 years declined from a high of 93 basis points at the end of January 1999 to 69 basis points in early March 1999. This is illustrated in **Figure 39**.

101. The historic lower liquidity in the Gilt, Sterling Swap, Agency and Mortgage Markets compared to the US accentuated the impact on certain occasions through the second half of 1998, and sterling swap spreads tended to lag the stabilisation compared to the US. Absolute rate sentiment (that is, all-in swap rates as opposed to Gilt yields and swap spreads evaluated on an individual basis) moved from anticipating an interest rate cut in early February 1999 (looking at a 50 basis point cut by mid-year) to negative, following Greenspan's comments in his Humphrey Hawkins Testament on 25 February. All-in 10-year swaps traded in a 5% to 5.35% range throughout the period.

Was the execution strategy of the hedges appropriate?

102 LCR long-term liabilities are the three fixed rate bond issues discussed in the bonds section above. However, its assets are a combination of floating rate cash deposits and a fixed rate debtor - Railtrack's commitment to purchase Section 1 of the Link. The hedging arrangements were put in place to mitigate the basis risk between LCR's assets and liabilities. The Central Case cashflow forecast was used. In theory, it would have been possible to remove this basis risk without the swap by partially funding the project with a floating rate instrument. However, the cost of issuing Floating Rate Notes or borrowing in the Euroloan market would have been far higher than the cost of the fixed rate funding plus the swap.

39 | **Swap spreads during first quarter of 1999**

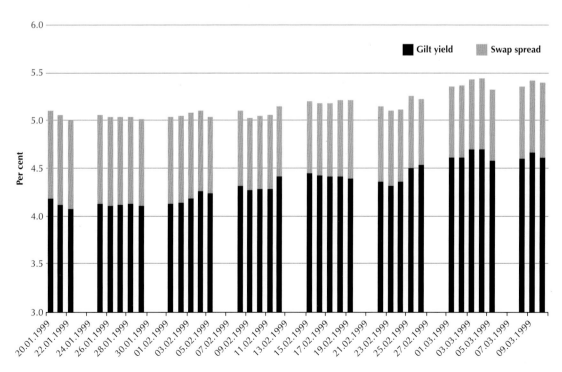

Source: RBC Dominion Securities

40 | Government Central Case: cash balance swap profile

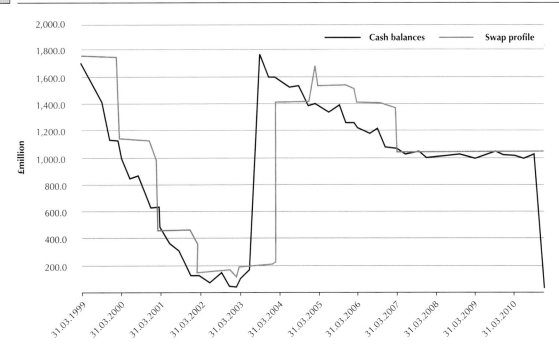

Source: RBC Dominion Securities

What was achieved?

103. The forecast residual cash balances were very closely matched with the swap profile. The net position involved LCR paying variable rates to the swap counterparty to balance with the variable receipts from surplus cash. LCR receives fixed rate payments. Assuming the Central Case holds, LCR will be largely interest rate neutral for the period which the swap hedge covers. **Figure 40** illustrates the match of the swap profile to the cash balances. We believe that structuring the swap package on a gross basis rather than just swapping a net cash position was the only way the hedge could be achieved with a high degree of accuracy.

What was not considered?

104. No consideration appears to have been given to the fact that the absolute fixed funding rates for creditworthy borrowers were at historic lows, in an inverted yield curve environment. A hedging strategy of this nature creates exposure (higher cost/lost benefit) to both higher variable versus long fixed interest rates and an upward shift in rates across the curve. Analysis of actual interest cost versus unhedged interest rate cost shows a significant advantage was foregone in favour of protecting against falling variable rates.

105. However, given the nature of the project, and the public sector funding at risk, we do not consider it unreasonable that the primary aim was the certainty of cashflow. If the project had been robust enough to borrow without the Government guarantee, we should expect private sector funders to have demanded a comprehensive hedging strategy which would have left little room for management to exploit movements in interest rates.

Were the costs of the swaps efficiently monitored and controlled?

106. We believe that there is one major area where the constraints imposed upon the banks may have limited their ability to achieve the best prices. This swap package was unusual in its size. We should, therefore, normally expect the banks involved to be given considerably more time to organise their books to manage the transactions in the most cost effective way. We have found no evidence of evaluation of the potential cost/saving of a gradual process of market-size hedge transactions, over a longer period of time, versus the need for confidentiality. We should expect the market to have an idea of what was going on, even if efforts were made to keep the arrangements confidential.

107. Nevertheless, given market conditions at the time and the complexity of the arrangements, we do not think any material competitive advantage would have been gained if more than two banks had been brought into the process. We also have some sympathy with the view that it was sensible to use banks who were familiar with the project and could therefore transact on a timely and efficient basis.

108. We concur with Schroder's opinion that the hedge transactions were being executed in relatively difficult market conditions, especially given the size. A number of decisions were taken to police and keep control of the process. These included:

   ■ limiting the transacting banks to only two;

   ■ imposed parameters regarding screen sources;

   ■ imposing limits on acceptable bid/offers outside screen indications;

   ■ Schroders overseeing the execution.

These were realistic measures to put in place.

109. We have been unable to determine the factors used in the choice of the two swap counterparties beyond their prior involvement with the project. Typical means of deciding on a choice of counterparty would include:

   ■ credit rating of the counterparty;

   ■ capabilities in the currency or product required (here GBP interest rate swaps);

   ■ involvement in the overall transaction. Award of swap business is frequently used to reward a bank for related work.

110. The area which seems inconsistent with the above related to the assessment of the capability of the counterparties. The absence of a sterling clearer (three of which are consistently ranked in the top five GPB counterparties) is surprising.

111. One way to reduce the costs of the hedge would have been to deliver the Gilts being sold by investors buying the 2010 GGBs on a switch basis to the swap counterparties to satisfy their positions arising from the hedge. We have been unable to fully verify the extent of this benefit (if any). We have also been unable to verify whether any possibility existed for influencing screen source pricing.

Annex 1 to Appendix 5   **Selected benchmarks for LCR Bonds**

Borrower	Nationality	Amount millions	Margin and Fees	Life	Purpose/remarks	Signing date
Red Nacional de Ferrocarriles Espanoles (RENFE)	Spain	SPT 45,000	Margin: 8bp, Participation Fee: 15bp for 1000m, 10bp for 500m	7 years	Proceeds are to refinance the Pta45bn loan arranged by Banco de Negocias Argentaria and CECA signed June 94.	8 Jan 97
Tagus Bridge	Portugal	DM 333	Margin: 162.5bp	13 years	Proceeds are to finance the design and construction of the new Tagus bridge and to maintain the existing bridge.	21 Feb 97
Kingdom of Spain	Spain	SPT 45,000	Margin: 7bp	7 years	Renegotiation of previous deal for Astilleros Espanoles SA.	6 Mar 97
Electricidade de Portugal SA (EdP)	Portugal	YEN 11,250	Margin: 12.50bp from 1 yr to 5 yrs, 15bp from 6 yrs to 7 yrs, Participation Fee: 10bp for 1200m, 7.50bp for 600m	7 years	Proceeds are to refinance a long-term loan signed in 1988. Oversubscribed but not to be increased.	12 Mar 97
Severn River Crossing Ltd	United Kingdom	STG 165	Margin: 75bp Participation fee: 30bp for 15m, 25bp for 10m	9 years	Refinancing of a £340m loan taken out in 1990. Syndication targeted at existing lenders. Oversubscribed but not increased.	25 Mar 97
ISAB Energy SpA	Italy	LIT 1,885,000	Margin 135bp Participation fee: 60bp for 100,000m, 50bp for 80,000m, 40bp for 50,000m, 30bp for 30,000m	13 years	Non-recourse project finance facility to construct an integrated power plant in Sicily. Oversubscribed but not increased.	16 May 97
Sarlux Srl	Italy	LIT 1,940,000	Margin 135bp from 1-5 yrs, 45bp from 6-8 yrs, 165bp from 9-15 yrs. Committment fee: 50bp, Participation fee 50bp for 60,000m, 40bp for 40,000m, 30bp for 20,000m	15 years	Limited-recourse project financing for an integrated power plant in Sardinia. Oversubscribed but not increased.	14 Jun 97
Saltend Cogeneration Co Ltd	United Kingdom	STG 72	Margin: 450bp	12 years	Project finance facility for the construction of a 1,200MW power plant. Project will sell 90% of its output directly into the English and Welsh electricity pool, taking full market risk.	14 Dec 97
Reseau Ferre de France (RFF)	France	FFR 4,000	Margin:5bp, Commitment Fee: 2bp Participation Fee: 3bp for 500m, 150bp for 300m	1 year	First-time borrower. Proceeds are for general corporate purposes. Split between a Ffr4bn 1-year revolving credit and a Ffr6bn 5-year revolving credit. The facility is also rated AAA by IBCA. It is 20% risk-weighted by the Commission Bancaire.	29 Dec 97
		FFR 6,000	Margin: 7bp, Commitment Fee: 3.5bp, Utilisation Fee: 2.50 bp for 50.00 to for 50.00 to 100.00% Fee: 3bp for 500m, 1.5bp for 300m	5 years	Targeted at core relationship banks. Oversubscribed by more than 60% but not increased.	
Autolink Concessionaires (M6) Ltd	United Kingdom	STG 230	Margin: 140bp, Participation Fee 45bp for 15m, 35bp for 10m	17 years	Proceeds are to finance the upgrade to motorway status of the M6 on both sides of the England/Scotland border. Project is last of current PFI trunk road upgrades and is under a 30 year contract.	Dec 1997
Ente Publico Radio Television Madrid-TeleMadrid	Spain	SPT 15,800	Margin: 9bp, Margin: 9bp, Commitment Fee: 10bp, Participation Fee: 4bp for 2000m, 2.50bp for 1000 to 2000m, 1.50bp for 500 to 1000m	5 years	Proceeds are to refinance a Pta 15.8bn arranged by Bank of America and signed 06-09-1994. Oversubscribed but not increased.	5 Feb 98

Borrower	Nationality	Amount millions		Margin and Fees	Life	Purpose/remarks	Signing date
Aeroports de Paris (ADP)	France	FFR	1,000	Margin: 10bp, Commitment Fee: 4.50bp for 50.00 Fee: 5.50bp , for 125m 2.50bp for 75 to 125m	5 years	The facility carries EPIC status, AAA ratings and a 20% risk-weighting. Replies by 02-12-1998. Fully underwritten by the arranger. Oversubscribed by more than 60% but not increased. Signed in counterpart.	4 Mar 98
Charbonnages de France	France	FFR	600	Margin: 13.50bp, Commitment Fee: 6.75bp, Utilisation Fee: 0bp for up to 50%, 2.50bp for 50 to 100%, Participation Fee: 7bp for 150m, 5.50bp for 100m, 3bp for 50m	5 years	Split between a Ffr 600m 5-year tranche and a Ffr 600m 1-year tranche. Oversubscribed but not increased.	28 Apr 98
		FFR	600	Margin: 12.50bp, Commitment Fee: 5bp, Utilisation Fee: 0bp for up to 50%, 2.50bp for 50 to 100%, Participation Fee: 7bp for 150m, 5.50bp for 100m, 3bp for 50m	1 year		
Radiotelevisione Italiana SpA (RAI)	Italy	Euro	150	Margin: 25bp, Commitment Fee: 12.50bp, Participation Fee: 10bp for 10m	5 years	First loan for an Italian borrower to be denominated in Euros. Proceeds are for general corporate purposes. Oversubscribed and increased from EUR100m to EUR150m.	23 Jul 98
Hellenic Republic	Greece	DM	220	Margin: 37.50bp, Commitment Fee: 20bp, Participation Fee 17.50bp for 30m, 15bp for 20m, 12.50bp for 10m.	8 years	Finances multi-purpose military vehicles. Targeted syndication. Oversubscribed but not increased.	31 Jul 98
Her Majesty in Right of Canada	Canada	US$	6,000	Margin: 4bp, Commitment Fee: 1.50bp, Facility Fee: 2.50bpa	5 years	Proceeds are for CP backstop.	8 Sep 98
Posten Norge BA	Norway	NKR	1,800	Margin: 14bp from 1 yr to 3 yrs, 16.50bp from 4 yrs to 5 yrs, 17.50bp from 6 yrs to 7 yrs, Commitment Fee: 7bp from 1 yr to 3 yrs, 8.25bp from 4 yrs to 5 yrs, 8.75bp from 6 yrs to 7 yrs, UF: 0bp for up	7 years	First-time borrower. Proceeds are for general corporate purposes and to refinance a state budget loan maturing end of 11-1998. There is a mandatory prepayment if state ownership falls below 100%	7 Oct 98

Annex 2 to Appendix 5

Indicative Secondary Market Yields 1998							
	Cades (France)	Republic of Ireland	Republic of Italy	Republic of Portugal	Kingdom of Spain	Kingdom of Sweden	Railtrack
Maturity	Jun-01	Jun-02	Apr-04	Mar-00	Jul-00	Jan-00	Oct-01
Margin (at issue)	0.0600	0.0700	0.0800	0.0775	0.0800	0.0800	0.2000
Jan 98	0.0659	0.0700	0.0800	0.0755	0.0800	0.0800	0.2427
Feb 98	0.0660	0.0700	0.0800	0.7933	0.0800	0.0800	0.2436
Mar 98	0.0631	0.0676	0.0784	0.0775	0.0757	0.0746	0.2447
Apr 98	0.0632	0.0676	0.0783	0.0775	0.0756	0.0743	0.2457
May 98	0.0665	0.0700	0.0783	0.0796	0.0800	0.0800	0.2555
Jun 98	0.0633	0.0700	0.0783	0.0776	0.0752	0.0737	0.2539
Jul 98	0.0634	0.0700	0.0783	0.0776	0.0750	0.0734	0.2553
Aug 98	0.0671	0.0830	0.0835	0.0776	0.0852	0.0870	0.2694
Sep 98	0.0745	0.0887	0.0836	0.0078	0.0909	0.1025	0.2810
Oct 98	0.0675	0.0809	0.0818	0.0778	0.0857	0.0880	0.2466
Nov 98	0.0716	0.0840	0.0818	0.0779	0.0920	0.0886	0.3028
Dec 98	0.0720	0.0786	0.0819	0.0777	0.0863	0.0800	0.3058

All figures are annual rates (per cent)

Annex 3 to Appendix 5

Gilt edged securities and bonds

1. A Gilt edged security ("Gilt") is a bond issued (nowadays) by the UK Treasury and backed by HM Government. It is a method of borrowing money, and Gilts form part of the National Debt. Gilts are in the form of securities and can, therefore, be bought and sold on a stock market. A holder of a Gilt earns a defined rate of interest, known as the coupon, on its face value and the Gilt will be redeemed (generally) at a specified future date at its face value. Most Gilts are redeemable on a specified date and carry a coupon at a fixed rate of interest. These Gilts are known as "Conventional Gilts".

2. Although the Government may issue bonds in various currencies, the term "Gilt" generally refers to securities denominated in sterling. Other borrowers, including foreign governments, local authorities, financial institutions and companies, borrow by issuing bonds which are traded in a similar way to Gilts.

3. As the Government is expected to pay all its debts in full and on the scheduled dates, when an investor buys a Gilt, he/she is making a "risk free" investment. When an investor chooses to buy a non-Gilt bond rather than a Gilt he/she may be assuming certain risks and will, therefore, expect to earn a higher return than by investing in Gilts. This additional return is called the "risk margin", or more colloquially, the "spread".

4. The risk margin will reflect a number of risks. Where the issuer is not considered as creditworthy as the Government, a large proportion of this margin compensates the investor for credit risk (the risk that the principal and coupon payments are not made in full and/or on time). The rest of the margin reflects a number of factors including relative supply and demand for the bond, market risks and liquidity (described below).

The return on Gilts and bonds

5. Gilts may trade in the market at above or below face value. As noted above, the coupon rate is often fixed. If prevailing interest rates are the same as the coupon payable on the Gilt, the Gilt should trade at its face value (known as "par" value). If prevailing rates are higher, the Gilt will tend to trade at below par and vice versa. This enables a purchaser of a Gilt with a non current coupon to invest with the immediate expectation that he can earn the prevailing rate of interest on this particular security. Bonds trade on a similar basis, the price reflecting the expected prevailing return for a bond with particular risks.

6. The rate of return an investor earns on a Gilt or bond, which takes into account the price the investor pays, the gross coupons payable, its maturity and the redemption amount is known as the gross redemption yield. The price of the Gilt or bond is a function of the gross redemption yield. It is the sum of the present value of all the future cashflows, discounted at the gross redemption yield. Therefore, when the gross redemption yield goes up, the price goes down and vice versa.

Yield curve

7. The gross redemption yields for Gilts with different redemption dates form a curve, known as the yield curve. The shape of this yield curve reflects a number of economic factors such as expectations of inflation and the likely direction of interest rates in the short term. However, the prices of Gilts and bonds are influenced by a number of other factors. These include:

    - supply and demand;

    - tax treatment of income and capital;

    - the size of the premium or discount at which the security trades to its par value;

    - relative size and/or age of issue;

    - special rights available to holders or unusual features;

    - eligibility for inclusion in a benchmark index.

8. All of these features may affect the price of a) all the securities in the market, b) those with a particular maturity or c) an individual bond or Gilt. In the Gilt market, it is possible to identify Gilts with characteristics set out above as the gross redemption yield does not lie on the yield curve (**Figure 41** overleaf).

41 **UK Gilts at 28 February 2000**

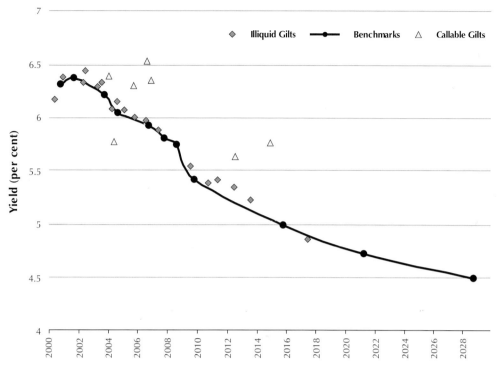

Source: RBC Dominion Securities

9. The liquidity of a security may be defined as the ease with which a buyer or seller can trade the security. A liquid security is often characterised as one where at a particular point in time, there is little difference between the price at which an amount of that security can be bought and that at which the same amount could be sold ("bid/offer spread"). In addition, the bid/offer spread for trading a large amount of the security will be similar for trading a smaller amount and will be consistent. It can be seen, therefore, that the relative demand for an issue will also affect liquidity.

10. Each of the factors described above, particularly the size of the issue, may have a positive or negative effect on the liquidity of a security. Generally, a small issue will be illiquid. However, a large issue may also become illiquid because of excess demand. In this case, the price will be high but the bid offer spread will be wide. This latter situation can be observed at the long end of the Gilt market, where excess demand for long dated Gilts by pension funds has driven up prices. The chronic shortage of Gilts has resulted in very poor liquidity at the long end.

11. In general, Gilts are very liquid. Non-government bonds or bonds issued by foreign governments are not as liquid because they are placed in smaller tranches. Liquidity is a very valuable characteristic to investors especially in volatile market conditions where liquidity tends to decrease. As a result, investors keep a large proportion of their portfolios in Gilts. If an investor expects a newly issued bond to be less liquid, he will expect a higher return. Apart from size of issue, other characteristics, such as an unusual repayment schedule, can also have a detrimental effect on liquidity. Therefore, two bonds identical in credit quality but of different sizes may trade at different prices. This can even be seen in the Gilt market, where certain smaller issues are illiquid and therefore have to offer a high return to investors (see **Figure 42**).

Performance risk

12. One of the features of a liquid bond, therefore, is that the price of that bond will tend to be higher than a bond which is identical except in terms of liquidity. Liquid bonds are therefore said to outperform illiquid bonds. Sterling bonds are bought and sold on the basis of relative value. When the price of one bond rises against another (or an index) with which it is compared, it is said to outperform. A number of factors affect performance including the period of measurement, the shape of the yield curve, liquidity and credit risk.

42 | **Capital amounts of outstanding gifts**

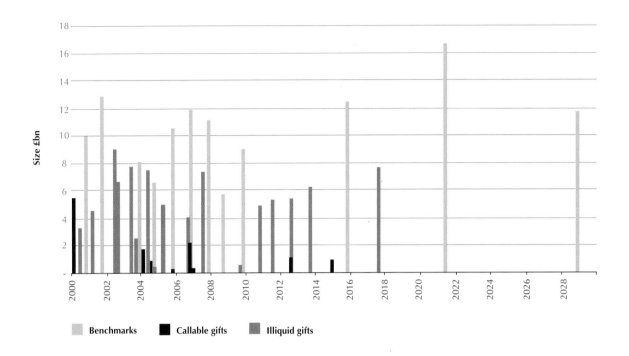

Source: RBC Dominion Securities

13. All corporate bonds are measured against the credit risk free rate earned on a Gilt, and the success of a fund's strategy may be evaluated in this way. There are also an increasing number of corporate bond indices which can also be used for performance measurement. When a fund manager considers buying a new investment, he/she will take into account the likelihood of the price of that bond outperforming the benchmark against which it is measured over a given period of time. The correlation of the bond to the constituents of the index will be very important but also the attitude of other investors in the market to the security.

14. The fund manager will therefore take into account a number of factors such as whether the bond has been fully placed at launch (supply matching demand), whether retail investors may buy the bonds at a later date and how many market makers are prepared to bid for and offer the bonds (liquidity). If there is doubt about these factors, the fund manager may still buy the bond but only at a lower price. Performance risk, therefore, can be said to affect a bond's price and be reflected in its risk margin.

Annex 4 to Appendix 5

The interest rate swap market

1. The interest rate swap market is, among other things, used to change the basis on which interest is paid on an asset or liability. Most commonly a floating rate is turned into fixed rate or vice versa. The fixed leg of the swap will be related to the Gilt market.

2. The swap market developed to allow borrowers who were not considered sufficiently creditworthy to access the fixed rate bond markets to lock into fixed rates of interest. As these borrowers usually borrowed from their banks (who understood their credit risk) swaps were and continue to be, generally intermediated by banks. As a result, the base swap rate (ie, the rate quoted before any corporate credit risk is taken into account) will itself reflect an interbank credit risk. This is generally considered to be an AA type risk.

3. The market convention is to quote a rate at which the bank will pay or receive a fixed or floating rate payment. This is the swap rate. The swap spread is the swap rate less the yield on the reference Gilt. Set out below is an example of a series of indicative swap rates as might be quoted on a broker's screen:

Maturity/Gilt	Swap Spreads (basis points)	Swap Rate (%)
4YR 6H Tr 03	+75/+70	6.87-6.8
5YR 6T Tr 04	+87/+82	6.79-6.7
6YR 8H Tr 05	+86/+81	6.71-6.6
7YR 7H 06	+87/+82	6.62-6.5
8YR 7Q 07	+90/+85	6.54-6.4
9YR 9 08	+88/+83	6.46-6.4
10Y 5T 09	+115/+110	6.39-6.3
12Y 8 13	+119/+113	6.30-6.2
15Y 8 15	+125/+117	6.15-6.0
20Y 8 21	+126/+114	5.94-5.8
25Y 8 21	+114/+102	5.82-5.7
30Y 6 28	+125/+113	5.73-5.6

4. At its simplest, this would mean, for example, at 5 years, that if a borrower borrowing floating rate money at LIBOR + 1% wanted to pay fixed rate on the loan, the borrower would pay the bank approximately 6.79% and receive back LIBOR. It can be said, therefore, that the borrower's cost of borrowing is fixed at 7.79% for 5 years (6.79% + 1%).

5. As noted, the swap rate is the rate at which a bank will receive a fixed rate payment from an interbank counterparty and pay LIBOR (or vice versa). If the bank is transacting the swap with a corporate, the bank will add several basis points to the swap rate to take into account the credit risk of its counterparty. If the fixed leg is being paid by a AA bank and the floating by a AAA counterparty, the AAA counterparty would expect to pay a lower floating rate than the interbank rate.

6. The swap spread, therefore, is considered to reflect relative credit risk. Other things being equal, as the swap spread widens (ie risk is increasing and credit is becoming more expensive), floating rate borrowing for AAA borrowers becomes cheaper if they raise fixed rate bonds in the bond market and swap them in the AA banking sector. (In fact, generally, bond spreads will widen to make sure this arbitrage does not become too great).

Appendix 6

Pricing of public transport services with high capital costs

1. Ordinarily, the social welfare maximising price for a transport service is where price equals marginal cost. At that level, transport services are provided up to the point at which the benefit of providing the last unit of service equals the cost of providing that unit of service.

2. However, some public transport schemes - particularly rail schemes - have high initial capital costs and, because of this, marginal cost pricing would lead to the scheme making a financial loss. **Figure 43** shows a simplified example where one price is charged for the transport service. The optimal level of service provision is where price equals marginal cost, PMC at point A. However, if the scheme were to be priced at this level, this would result in a financial loss equal to the shaded area B. The Average Cost, which includes the initial fixed costs, is greater than the Marginal Cost of providing the last unit of service, so a financial loss results. The scheme would break even if Average Cost pricing PAC were adopted, point C. But this would mean that $D_{MC} - D_{AC}$ potential rail travellers would be priced off, despite the fact they are willing to pay the additional costs they impose, so this is a less efficient level of service provision. This is the type of situation where the Government may take the welfare decision to pay a grant for the initial fixed costs to allow the operator to price efficiently, or to subsidise the operation of the service in order to prevent the operator making a loss.

43 | **Pricing a public transport project with declining costs**

Pricing at Marginal Cost, point A leads to financial loss, area B. Pricing at Average Cost, point C deters $D_{MC} - D_{AC}$ potential travellers

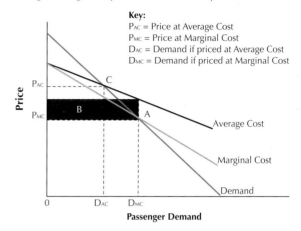

Key:
P_{AC} = Price at Average Cost
P_{MC} = Price at Marginal Cost
D_{AC} = Demand if priced at Average Cost
D_{MC} = Demand if priced at Marginal Cost

Source: National Audit Office

Appendix 7

Financial and cost-benefit analysis framework

This appendix explains the method the Department used to calculate the benefits and costs of the Link. It explains the numbers in **Figure 19** of the main text, showing the May 1998 value for money assessment of the Link, based on Government Central Case patronage forecasts.

1. In summary, the framework for the Department's value for money assessment was as follows:

	Total Costs	(Capital and Operating Costs)
Less	Total Revenues	(Financial Benefits)
=	**Funding Gap**	(Amount of public sector contribution for which bidder bids)
plus	Total Non-financial Benefits	(User plus Non-User Benefits)
=	**Net Present Value**	

These terms are explained below.

2. If the net present value is greater than zero, then the project can be judged to be economically justified, though a reasonable margin for error is usually allowed due to uncertainties in estimation methods and passenger forecasts. What is judged to be a reasonable margin will depend on the size of the project. The net present value takes no account of other impacts, which are not quantified in monetary terms in the value for money assessment, but are still important impacts of the project.

3. The economic justification for a public transport scheme such as the Link depends on a combination of financial and cost-benefit analysis. The financial analysis establishes the degree of commercial viability of the scheme by comparing the discounted stream of expected revenues with that of expected costs over the appraisal period, in this case up to 2052. As explained in Appendix 6, a major rail infrastructure project such as the Link involves enormous capital cost for construction and it is seldom the case that the initial investment can be recovered through fare revenues alone. The difference between the financial results of total expected revenues and total expected costs is the "Funding Gap". This is the amount of public sector support for which the private sector bidder bids.

4. In order to justify the decision to provide public support to the Link, the Department attempted to estimate the level of welfare benefits such support would be purchasing. These are generally benefits for which no market exists, but which are judged to represent benefits to society. The assessment then uses a form of cost-benefit analysis to quantify these benefits in order to judge whether they are sufficient to cover the funding gap and justify Government support for the project.

5. The Department, in agreement with the Treasury, decides which benefits can be counted in monetary terms towards a transport project's economic justification. In the case of the Link, the then Department of Transport included passenger benefits for rail passengers resident in the UK, travelling on Eurostar UK international services and on new domestic services. These were based mainly on increases in consumers' surplus (see below) due to estimated capacity improvements and time savings. There is no UK precedent for including international user benefits for a rail project, as this is the first scheme for which they could be considered relevant.

Benefits

Increases in consumers' surplus

6. Consumers' surplus arises where there is a difference between what consumers of a service or product are willing to pay and what they actually pay. So those who would be willing to pay more will benefit from the service by the amount of the difference between what they would be willing to pay and what they actually pay. It is not usually practical for an operator to devise a price structure which would enable it to capture precisely the benefit that each passenger derives from using the service. For example, the information costs the operator would need to incur to devise and implement a pricing structure which discriminated sufficiently to allow this and the practicalities of its implementation would be prohibitive.

7. A certain amount of price discrimination between different groups of passengers is possible, and more can be charged to groups which are less responsive to higher prices. For example, much higher fares are charged for first class than standard class passengers. Although these are effectively different products, as the type of service is different for the two classes, first class travellers are often business travellers who are less responsive to changes in price than leisure travellers. Business travellers are, therefore, often charged at a higher rate than is required to cover the additional costs of the greater level of service they receive.

8. The Department estimated changes in consumer surplus for UK resident international passengers. It estimated the benefits due to the increased rail capacity the Link would provide and the benefits due to time savings resulting from faster journey times. The total cost of travel includes money costs, such as fares, but also includes the cost of the time spent travelling, waiting etc. These all form the "generalised cost" of travel. A reduction in journey time reduces the generalised cost of travel and should increase demand, all other things being equal. The expected level of international benefits accruing as a result of the Link were based on a method for calculating consumers' surplus known as the "rule of half". Those passengers who use Eurostar UK before the Link opens get the full value of the capacity and time saving benefits, and those switching to the service only get half of the value (**Figure 44**). To incorporate the increases in consumers' surplus into the Department's value for money assessments, the annual changes in consumers' surplus compared with the "no Channel Tunnel Rail Link" scenario were discounted at 6 per cent a year after inflation to 1997 over the assessment period. The sum of these annual figures gave the total figure for international and domestic passenger benefits.

| 44 | **The Rule of Half** |

Before the Link is built, the generalised cost of travel on Eurostar UK (fares plus travel time and other costs) is P and the number of trips made at this level of cost is Q. At this level, the consumer surplus is the area PDR, as those passengers on the demand line would be prepared to incur higher generalised costs to travel, so benefit from having lower costs than they are prepared to pay.

After the Link opens, the reduction in journey times and the relief of capacity constraints (thus meaning lower fares) reduce the generalised cost of travel on Eurostar UK to P_1. As a result of the lower costs, other things being equal, more passengers will be attracted to travel, so demand increases to Q_1.

The fall in generalised costs, therefore, increases total consumer surplus to P_1R_1D. Those who travelled before, OQ, benefit from the full increase, so their consumer surplus rises by PP_1SR.

Those who have switched to Eurostar UK following the reduction in generalised costs, QQ_1, however, were not prepared to incur the previous higher costs of P (point T), so on average only benefit from half of the increase in consumer surplus between Q and Q_1, which is the area RR_1S. This is the rule of the half.

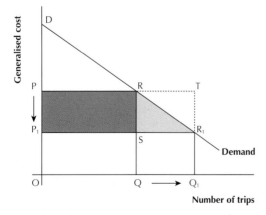

Capacity benefits

9. Capacity benefits are said to arise because the Link increases rail capacity from 19.2 million to 34.2 million passengers a year, which is around the capacity of the Channel Tunnel. In the absence of the Link, the Department estimates that growth in patronage would mean that the 19.2 million passenger capacity would be exceeded by around 2025. Further increases in demand would then need to be suppressed by increasing fares. When the Link is operating, the increased capacity will mean that there is no need to increase fares, so those travelling will benefit from lower fares than they would if the Link were not built.

10. Total Capacity benefits are the increases in fares per passenger multiplied by the number of passengers travelling in the no-Link case. The first 19.2 million passengers get the full benefit of not having to pay the increased fare, and the passengers in excess of 19.2 million get half the benefit, in keeping with the "rule of half". These benefits are effectively cash benefits to passengers, unlike the resource benefits represented by the bulk of the user benefits, time savings.

Time saving benefits

11. Time saving benefits arise because transport is a means and not an end. People do not generally travel for travel's sake, but in order to get somewhere to do something from which they derive benefits. The longer the time spent travelling, the less time they will have to enjoy the activity at the destination. People show that they are willing to pay to save time by, for example, choosing to fly abroad rather than take a slower mode, even though in the past flying may have been more expensive in money terms. A transport project which leads to a reduction in journey times therefore provides benefits to those using it. The Department has standard values of time which are applied to calculate the value of time saving benefits. Different values have been calculated for working and non-working time, as people travelling in work time tend to place a higher value on time savings than those travelling at their leisure.

12. For the Link, the Department commissioned consultants to estimate specific values of time for business and leisure passengers. The time savings are expected to be around 33 minutes per international trip to and from St. Pancras, and around 20 minutes per trip for journeys to and from Waterloo. Domestic benefits were estimated by the Office of Passenger Rail Franchising. This used values of time and the bidders' estimates of levels of patronage and provision of domestic services. The benefits include an element of relief from overcrowding and improvements in reliability, but the bulk of the domestic benefits is represented by time savings.

Non-user transport benefits

Road decongestion

13. These benefits arise from the fact that the Link will reduce rail journey times on some routes, thus reducing the generalised cost of travelling by train. This will make rail travel more competitive with travel by road in congested peak conditions, so there will be some switching to rail, known as "Modal Switching".

14. Modal switching reduces road traffic flows and hence reduces road journey times. This brings time savings to those who remain on the road network, and it is these that are reflected in the £30 million figure. This was estimated in a 1993 Union Railways Ltd report. The small amount of road decongestion benefits included reflects the fact that there is probably little scope for modal switching from cars on the routes for which domestic services will run. The Department was unable to locate the detailed calculations of the figure, so we have not been able to verify this.

Environmental benefits from freight transfer

15. The Department does not usually apply money values to environmental impacts and improvements resulting from transport schemes, with the exception of assessing applications for Rail Freight Grants . Here, it must be shown that freight will transfer from road to rail, thus bringing about environmental benefits. Benefit values are assigned to lorry kilometres according to the type of road from which the freight is expected to transfer. The Department expects the Link to reduce congestion on existing rail routes by increasing rail capacity and consider that this will make rail freight more attractive, particularly between Ashford and the Tunnel. The 1993 Union Railways Ltd report also estimated expected freight transfer, but the Department could not locate the detailed calculations. We have therefore not been able to verify this figure.

Regeneration benefits

16. In the past, the Department's policy on regeneration benefits was that there is no clear and agreed methodology for calculating monetary estimates for transport projects, so these benefits should not be included directly in transport scheme appraisals. The estimated impact of a project on an area of regeneration priority should, however, be taken into account as part of the project appraisal. In the case of the Link, the Department decided that monetary estimates should also be included.

17. In this case, the Housing and Urban Economics Division (HUE) of the Department used a "dual-track" methodology. This employed two different methods to estimate the regeneration impacts of the Link. The Department estimated:

- The impact of the Link on development values in the main areas affected (King's Cross, Stratford and Ebbsfleet); and,

- The main regeneration outputs and outcomes associated with the Link and what the Government would have to pay to achieve these by more traditional regeneration funding programmes, such as the Single Regeneration Budget Challenge Fund or through English Partnerships.

45 | **The percentage split of estimated jobs created by the Link**

The figure shows the estimated percentage split of jobs between the four regeneration areas

Area	Percentage of estimated jobs created
King's Cross	6.5
Stratford	30
Ebbsfleet	61
Royal Docks	2.5
Total	**100**

Source: The Department

18. The Department estimated the number of jobs it believed the Link would create directly or through development in the regeneration areas through which it passes. This produced an estimate of some 50,000 additional jobs (80,000 gross). These were split between four main areas (**Figure 45** shows the percentage of the total estimated in each area).

19. The Department then estimated the cost of creating this number of jobs through other regeneration programmes, using a range of costs per job associated with these programmes. This gave an estimate of £1,000 million for the Government's "willingness to pay" to create this number of jobs.

20. One impact of economic growth or development is an increase in the number of trips being made. These trips should already be reflected in the traffic forecasts, so will be reflected in the calculations of increases in passenger's consumer surplus discussed earlier in this appendix. However, the inclusion of a separate figure for regeneration benefits risks double counting of these benefits. For this reason, the Department removed 50 per cent of the estimated regeneration benefits, as most of the benefits to UK residents would already be reflected in the value for money assessment of international passenger benefits. The final figure included in the assessment was therefore £500 million as an estimate of the regeneration impacts of non-UK resident passengers and other local regeneration impacts.

THE CHANNEL TUNNEL RAIL LINK

Reduced Thameslink 2000 benefits

21. The Link includes some work, mainly at St. Pancras station, which ties in with the Thameslink 2000 rail project. The fact that the Link is now due to open in late 2006, rather than 2003 as planned in the original deal means that there have been delays to the benefits the Department estimates will arise from Thameslink 2000. These have been included at £100 million.

Costs

London Underground Limited and A2/M2 roadwork costs. The Link increases the costs of other projects concerning London Underground Ltd and the A2/M2, and these costs are not included in the estimates of the Link's construction costs. So these costs are represented separately at £170 million.

Government grants. This is the main public sector contribution to the Link, in the form of Capital and Deferred grants and Domestic Capacity Charges. The total figure of £1,800 million has been rounded and is net of Land rental payments to the Government.

Additional support. This is the estimated call on the Access Charge loan, under the Government Central Case of £140 million.

Office of Passenger Rail Franchising (OPRAF) subsidy. OPRAF estimates that the Link will lead to increased subsidies to domestic passenger services. OPRAF estimated the additional amount of subsidy using its computer modelling techniques and provided this for the Department. After taking account of the phasing of the Link's construction, the estimated amount is £250 million.

Eurostar UK revenue foregone. If the Government had not accepted the restructured deal, Eurostar UK would have reverted to public sector operation. Over the assessment period, the Department estimated that Eurostar UK would earn net revenues of £440 million. This was included as a cost, as the Government gave up these net revenues by accepting the deal.

Eurostar UK debt payments avoided. If the Government had not accepted the restructured deal and Eurostar UK had reverted to public sector operation, then the Government would have been liable to repay Eurostar UK's debts. The Government avoided these repayments of an estimated £400 million by accepting the deal.

Thameslink 2000 work avoided. The costs of the project include works for Thameslink 2000 at St. Pancras. The Department assumed that this would have to be funded from another public source if the Link did not go ahead, at an estimated cost of £240 million.

Project wind up costs. The Department would have incurred costs if the restructured deal had not been accepted and the Link had been shelved. These would have arisen from net property costs (the discounted sum of purchase and rental cashflows), and the cost of the orderly wind up of the project to the point where it could be reused at a later date, with drawings signed off and catalogued. This gave an estimated total of £110 million.

Appendix 8

The key benefits and costs included in the National Audit Office value for money assessment of the Link

This appendix explains the figures used in Figure 20 of the main text, where the National Audit Office re-worked the Department's value for money assessment. The figures are based on the Government Central Case forecasts of patronage.

Benefits

International passenger benefits

Time savings

These are based on time savings of 20 minutes from 2003-2007 and for the whole assessment period for Waterloo passengers, who will only benefit from Section 1 time savings. One third of trains/passengers are assumed by the Department to use Waterloo after Section 2 opens. The Department and the National Audit Office assumed different levels of time savings for Section 2. The assessment of time savings has changed as the specification of the Link developed, reflecting time tabling assessments of running speeds, stopping patterns and the Link's operational capacity. The Department's estimate of time savings was based on an engineering assessment from July 1996, which concluded that Section 1 would deliver a time saving of 20 minutes, and Section 2 a further time saving of 19 minutes. Only two thirds of passengers were assumed to benefit from the Section 2 time saving, therefore, the Department used a weighted time saving of 30 minutes for all passengers.

The National Audit Office calculations assumed time savings for Section 2 of 13 minutes, and total time savings of 33 minutes for St. Pancras passengers from 2007 onwards. This was consistent with LCR's assumptions in the "LCR Key Assumptions Book" of June 1998, when the restructured deal was announced. The Department has now told us that the latest Section 2 timetables have revised average time savings from Section 2 of 17.5 minutes.

Value of time growth assumptions have been corrected. The growth rate was 2.4% a year in the Department's version. We have used the growth rates in the Department's guidance note, Highways Economics Note 2: ie 2.07% until 2016, and 2.21% a year thereafter.[19] For time savings and capacity benefits the rule of half applies, so those "existing passengers" (ie up to 19.2 million) get the full benefit (Appendix 7, **Figure 44**). Those above that only get half of the benefit.

Domestic passenger benefits

The Office of Passenger Rail Franchising figure has been input, at £800 million. This takes account of the fact that the link is to be phased, that is, built in two sections. The Department had used a figure of £1 billion, which did not take account of the phasing.

Road decongestion benefits

These have been adjusted to take account of phasing of construction as in the Department's central case. They stand at £30 million (although we have not seen the detailed calculations supporting the figure).

Environmental freight benefits

The Department believes that these accrue to Section 1 of the Link, as a result of the relief of rail congestion, mainly between the Channel Tunnel and Ashford. The Department estimated benefits of £90 million, but again we have not seen the detailed calculation of this figure.

Regeneration benefits

These are estimated at £500 million by the Department, as explained in Appendix 7.

Reduced Thameslink 2000 benefits.

The Department had originally included a figure of £200 million for the impact of a delay in opening the Link on the benefits of the Thameslink 2000 project. This was removed from the final assessment as there had been a two year delay in Thameslink 2000 anyway. However, the Department's April 1998 assessment stated that the delay to the Link was three years, so we have included an impact of £100 million on the Thameslink 2000 benefits as an estimate of the increased delay.

---

19   *Highways Economics Note 2 is used as guidance in the appraisal of road schemes. The rate of growth of the value of time in the note applies to the whole economy so is also applicable in the case of the Link.*

Costs

London Underground Limited King's Cross Northern ticket hall and A2/M2 roadwork costs. These were originally £130 million, but the Department removed them from the final assessment as it was considered that work would need to be done even in the absence of the Link. However, the original assessment states that these works are specifically to fit in with the Link. Following discussions with the Department, the figure has been reinstated and increased to £170 million.

Government grants etc. The direct grants are £2,100 million, partially offset by expected land rentals from 2030 with a present value of £300 million, giving a net figure of £1,800 million.

Additional support. The Deputy Prime Minister's announcement in June 1998 gave a figure of £140 million in the Government Central Case. The Department's final assessment rounded this down to £100 million. We have used the correct figure of £140 million.

Office of Passenger Rail Franchising (OPRAF) subsidy. This has been taken from an OPRAF paper in June 1998. It quotes a figure of £250 million after taking account of the impacts of phased construction, rather than the unphased £400 million included in the Department's assessment.

Eurostar UK revenue foregone. The Department figure of £440 million has been retained as no other estimates are available.

Eurostar UK debt payments avoided. Debt repayments avoided have been included at £400 million.

Thameslink 2000 work avoided. The costs of the project include works for Thameslink 2000 at St. Pancras. The Department assumed that this would have to be funded from another public source if the Link did not go ahead. We have retained the Department's estimated costs of £240 million.

Project wind up costs. The Department's figure of £110 million has been retained.

Reports

Reports by the Comptroller and Auditor General, Session 2000-2001

The Comptroller and Auditor General has to date, in Session 2000-2001, presented to the House of Commons the following reports under Section 9 of the National Audit Act, 1983:

Culture, Media and Sport
Access to the Victoria and Albert Museum ....HC 238

Defence
Maximising the benefits of defence equipment ....HC 300
co-operation

Education
Education Action Zones:
Meeting the Challenge - the lessons identified
from auditing the first 25 Zones ....HC 130
Improving Student Performance:
How English further education colleges can
improve student retention and achievement ....HC 276

Environment
Inland Flood Defence ....HC 299

General Topics
1999-2000 General Report of the Comptroller
and Auditor General...HC 25-XIX

HM Customs and Excise
Regulating Freight Imports from
Outside the European Community ....HC 131

Modernising Government
Modernising Construction...HC 87
Measuring the Performance of Government ....HC 301
Departments

National Health Service
The National Blood Service ....HC 6
Tackling Obesity in England ....HC 220
Educating and Training the Future Health
professional workforce in England ....HC 277

Public Private Partnerships
The Radiocommunications Agency's
joint venture with CMG ....HC 21
The Re-negotiation of the PFI-type deal for the
Royal Armouries Museum in Leeds........................HC 103
The financial analysis for the London Underground
Public Private Partnerships ....HC 54
The Channel Tunnel Rail Link ....HC 302

Privatisation/Asset Sales
The Sale of Part of the UK Gold Reserves ....HC 86

Regulation
Giving Domestic Customers a Choice
of Electricity Supplier ....HC 85

Revenue Departments
Petroleum Revenue Tax...HC 5

Social Security
The Medical Assessment of Incapacity and
Disability Benefits...HC 280

Transport
Ship Surveys and Inspections ....HC 338

Printed in the UK for The Stationery Office on behalf of the
Controller of Her Majesty's Stationery Office
Dd.5069852, 3/01, 5673, Job No. TJ003882